Ocean of Smiles, Stream of Tears

Ocean of Smiles, Stream of Tears

A Memoir on the Ebbs and Flows of Life

A Memoir

by
Ruthell Cook Price

Order this book online at www.trafford.com
or email orders@trafford.com

Most Trafford titles are also available at major online book retailers.

Printed in the United States of America.

ISBN: 978-1-4269-5256-2 (sc)

Trafford rev. 01/24/2012

 www.trafford.com

North America & International
toll-free: 1 888 232 4444 (USA & Canada)
phone: 250 383 6864 ♦ fax: 812 355 4082

TABLE OF CONTENTS

In Memory
This book is dedicated to my parents, Burnie and Ardie
Mae "Honey" Cook
Hazel Anderson, mentor of 50 years
Mary Elizabeth Blackmon, our "Sugga"
Elena and Angela Aguiar
Lester Bernard Evans

This book is dedicated to
My Sons: Channing and Lladon
Grandchildren: Jordan Ky and Alexandria Rachelle
My Step Children: Eric, Martine and Jonathan

Acknowledgements
Special thanks to:
Christine Brooks Martin, Editor
Judith Echols, Marsha Echols and Mark Price, Final
Manuscript Team
To:
Debra Cook, Georgia Williams, Joyce Ann Holmes and
My Church Family, California Harvest Tabernacle
Bible Church
Thank you for your encouragement.

Introduction

A copy of "Chicken Soup for the Mother's Soul," publication was given to me as a Christmas gift in 1997, from a friend Micki. Her husband purchased the book for her, thinking it was a book of recipes for chicken soup. She loved the book and thought that I would also and I did.

Years passed and one day an author and friend, Rick Mizuno, forwarded an email to me soliciting stories for "Chicken Soup for the African American Woman's Soul." I held on to the email for three months.

In the meantime, while serving for over 30 years, as associate minister /executive assistant at Harvest Tabernacle Bible Church under the auspices of our pastor, Bishop Donald R. Cook, Sr., time after time, I was asked to fill in for him during his absence by presenting Sunday morning messages. I would always include several personal experiences or stories someone would have shared with me. One Sunday following one of my presentations, one of the young ladies of the church named Phyllis said to me, "You are full of stories!"

One day I ran across Rick's email and Phyllis' statement hit me and I thought, Wow, I do have stories that I'd love to share. That very day I began to write. The following week was the submission deadline. I submitted three stories to editor, Eve Hogan. From hundreds of submissions for "Chicken Soup for the African American Woman's Soul" publication, one of my three, "Bus Vouchers," was selected by Lisa Nichols, author. With those odds, I thought, I had procrastinated long enough and I must write. As for authors Rick, Eve and Lisa, well they are my "Get Ready, Get Set, Go Team!"

After completing this book, I realized that I had actually began to learn the significance of prayer first by watching my parents pray and wait for results. But by the age of 7 (see "Classmates") prayer became real for me.

As I reflect, prayer became generational because my son Lladon prayed at age 7 as well for something very special in his life (see "Kodak Moment"). Allow me to close by saying "Prayer Works!"

CHAPTER ONE

IN THE BEGINNING

Off to California They Go

My parents met in Waelder, Texas when they were in their early twenties. Mom often told me that she agreed to marry my dad because he was one of the few young men who would work and maintain a good job. So she said yes!

Their weekend activity would be daddy driving mom to a neighboring city's restaurant that specialized in tamales. Dad's motorcycle had a side car that mom had no problems riding in.

My father was a presser at the Hilton Hotel in Texas in their dry cleaning department. He apparently was good at it because his boss had grown to really like him as well as his work.

One day he called my father into his office and asked him if he would consider moving west to California. He informed him that the Long Beach Hilton had an opening for a presser and he wanted to recommend him for the position. My father discussed it with my mother and after much pondering she finally agreed to go. Daddy rode his motorcycle to California and mommy came on the train a couple of weeks later.

Both were born in Texas and had lived there all their lives, she with her grandparents and dad with his older sister and father. Dad's mother, Addie passed away when he was very young. My mother was an only child born to a young single mother named Mattie. Her grandparents refused to give her up and she remained with them until she was 14 years old. She would tell me how hard she worked on the farm, helping to raise her younger cousins, while their parents picked cotton.

Her clothing items were always hand me downs from older cousins. She shared with me once that her mother sent her a box of new dresses, only to have her grandmother give the prettiest ones to her cousins. I think that's what broke the camels back.

One day she secretly wrote to her mother, who had moved to the big city, I have no idea which one, asking if she could please come to live with her. Her mother agreed and the date was set and her train ticket was to be at the station. All she had to do was remember the date and have Grandpa hitch up the horse and buggy to get her to the station on time to hear the conductor say, "All aboard."

Well she remembered the date and thought she started in enough time to get to the station but that particular day Grandpa was slower than ever before. Mom said she begged him to move faster but Grandpa refused. It was deliberate. He didn't want to lose her. She had been his nurse, housekeeper, bookkeeper, and babysitter for his other grandchildren. She milked cows and fed chickens, babies and pre-teens daily.

Grandpa was a very tall, slender man with an olive complexion, and straight hair, because he was of Mescalero Apache descent. He was the pastor of two churches in two towns that were nearby. On the weekends she would accompany him to church services and lead the congregation in hymns. Whenever called, she would assist her grandmother, the local midwife, with delivering babies. Her grandmother, who was White, couldn't read or write so my mother would sign all documents for her from age eleven to fourteen.

She would laugh and tell me that her signature was on most of the birth certificates in their local Hall of Records. She only got as far as the sixth grade in school, but could add, subtract and multiply faster than most people I knew, me for sure!

After missing the train the first time, Grandpa managed to get her to the station the second time, which was about two weeks later. She shared how she cried those two weeks longing to be with her mother and to get away from the Preacher and the Midwife.

Once she left her grandparents home, she vowed she would never return and she didn't. We were never taken to Texas for family reunions or vacations. She wouldn't even return for funerals, but she would send money and her regards. She kept her word to never, ever return to that awful place because the memory of her childhood made her sick. Hers was so awful that she often said that if she ever had children their lives would be completely different from hers and it was. We traveled, had very few chores and never went without food or new clothes.

My parents moved to Long Beach, California in 1940, and my oldest brother Lloyd, was born one year later. They remained in Long Beach for two years until my father obtained another pressing job in Huntington Park. So they moved to Los Angeles into the Pueblo Del Rio Project community and there in 1943 is where my brother Donald was born. And my mother, no longer the teenage midwife's assistant, was told to have a midwife because it was the way to go, to not have the expense of a hospital. By the time I came along in 1950, it was no longer in vogue to give birth to your children at home, so I was born at White Memorial Hospital.

We lived in the Pueblo until 1953. I can remember my mother often telling the story of why she was one of the first in the Pueblo to purchase a television set. A short time after they were invented, two of the community residents purchased sets for their families. They would allow as many children into their living rooms as possible. All the children in the Pueblo would gather at these two residences hoping to be a part of the group allowed inside. Those who were not able to enter would stand in front of the bay windows of the apartments to watch shows like "Howdy Doody" and "I Love Lucy."

One day my brothers were among those who didn't make it inside. For some reason the lady of the house pulled the shade down on her bay window, blocking all view of the TV. My mother just happened to be looking out of her window for my brothers at that time and saw what had occurred, and felt that her sons had been mistreated. All the children that were outside went home disgruntled and hurt.

That same evening when my father arrived home from work, my parents were off to Gold's Furniture Store to purchase our first television set. It was purchased "on time", meaning small monthly installments until paid in full—for those of you under the age of 40. Credit cards as we know them today were not in existence in the 50s. Monthly payments, save for months, an open account with the store (on time) and cash payments were the ways in which furniture, clothing and appliances were purchased.

Our First Home

I can remember the day we moved from the Pueblo into our first home. Although I was only three years old, I remember being carried by my grandmother's brother, Uncle Bill, into this large place with stuff all over the living room floor. Uncle Bill and his wife Cora, had been caring for me for several days while my parents were making the move. I was sat down in the middle of all the stuff and amazed at the size of the place. I just sat and looked around for what seemed like forever.

My parents purchased a residence that had three businesses attached to the boulevard side of the property. We could walk out of our kitchen into one side of the rental property and from one of the bedrooms into the other side of the property. It was huge. Our parents took the plunge, like so many Blacks at the time, and started their own dry cleaning business which they maintained from 1953 to 1963. My mother would write up the customers and my father would press the clothes. He taught my mother how to sew torn clothing and brush sweaters. She also learned how to cover for him when the clothes weren't ready.

After several years of making a decent income, business began to slow down, which caused my father to worry and begin to drink. Clothes were beginning to now be made from fabrics that didn't require dry cleaning. Washing machines did the trick.

Daddy became one of the independent alcoholics in the neighborhood. Several of his community friends would meet up at the cleaners to discuss the good old days. All retired except him. As he pressed clothes, they would come to chat and offer to run to the store as he worked, hoping he would say yes. They knew that if he would accept their offer, drinks would be on him. This went on for quite a while. Payments on the shop equipment went into default because daddy spent the earnings on spirits from the corner store.

Mother's breaking point came one day and as my father was upstairs in bed sleeping off one of his binges, she contacted the company that they were purchasing the equipment from and requested that they come immediately to pick it up. Everything was picked up that day.

By the time my father woke up everything had been taken out of the cleaners. I was thirteen and afraid that once he woke up and was told that he was out of business, he would react violently. However, he wasn't a violent man and he considered all that mother had gone through trying to maintain things. He realized that she had no other alternative to sustaining our family.

Subsequently, they rented out two sections of the rental property and acquired jobs outside of the home. One was rented as a TV repair shop, the other a beauty salon but the third remained empty for several months. I can recall a specific occurrence regarding the rental of the third store. It was when my brother Donald had acquired an athletic scholarship for Track and Field from Grambling College. There were no funds for his flight or miscellaneous needs. He went to our mother hoping for some form of assurance that the funds would appear in time for him to accept the scholarship. Mother being a woman of prayer and faith said to him, "If I rent the store within the next few days, I will give you the money for school." Donald walked away in despair thinking, "Oh well, there goes school." But mother prayed and her faith stood tall and strong. Often my brothers and I would walk by her bedroom, only to see her on her knees praying. What was ironic to me was that daddy prayed every night before he went to bed. We would tease him by saying, "Daddy you pray every night but won't go to church." People just prayed during the fifties, I guess. We knew very little about faith and belief. This situation was to be my second experience of seeing the hand of God. My first is explained in the next story, "Growing Pains."

After a few days of mother fasting and praying, a lady who lived on the other end of the block came over and asked mother if she could rent the store as a storage facility for her furniture. She wanted to move back home to care for her mother but had no place to store her furniture and she was prepared to pay several months in advance. Now mother had enough money to give Donald for college. He left two weeks later breaking world records during his freshman year on Grambling College's track team. This was one of several occurrences that drew me closer to Christ. I thought, "Wow, if He could do this for my brother, and me being the better behaved child, what He would do for me!

My parents never fought nor disrespected one another. My mother maintained her religion from childhood, until her death. My father wouldn't set foot in a church, not even on holidays, but he never stood in the way of her attending or taking the three of us with her. It just gave him more time to drink. She believed in the scripture that, "A sanctified wife would sanctify her husband," so she continued to take us to church and served as an untiring saint.

After completing Pepperdine University, majoring in Religion with a stint as chaplain for the Los Angeles

County Sheriff's Department in 1976, my brother Donald was called back to his birthplace to start a ministry and organize a church in the Pueblo Del Rio Project Community. After being a member of the Mount Olive Church of God in Christ for over forty years, my mother left to assist him.

Donald was kind enough to allow her to name the church and Harvest Tabernacle Church, Inc. was born. I tagged along to keep them company, including my husband and sister-in-law, Claudine.

Mother had worked in several capacities at Mount Olive Church but was known as one of their main fundraising coordinators. Our pastor, the late Bishop E. B. Stewart would call her whenever the finances of the church needed a boost. No, he wouldn't call the deacons, he would call our mother. She would always ask him to give her two or three days before getting back to him with a plan. During this time, she would fast, pray and wait for a plan from God that would allow her to raise funds to enable the church to get caught up with its expenses. She never failed in her efforts because the plan was always from God.

At Harvest Church she served as the church consultant for 10 years prior to retiring. Donald and I would often jokingly call her the "insulting consultant" of the church. She had a way of dealing with any given situation. But she was kind and people loved her to the point that they would accept anything she presented to them, like "baby your skirt is too tight or too short," "sweetie it's time for a girdle," or "brother, stop chasing that young lady!" Those without clothes to wear to church would be issued one of her credit cards to go shopping. Everyone loved her.

She continued to stand on the word of God as she prayed daily for our father. One Sunday our father showed up at church. He rode into the parking lot on his motorcycle, and most people were unaware of who he was. The parking attendant pointed out a space on the lot for him. When he walked into the sanctuary, I think my brother may have thought he was seeing things.

I was in the choir loft and I thought I was seeing things. The power of God and how he answers prayer was more than I could explain! After the third visit, when my brother (opened the doors of the church) invited guests to become members, our father was the first one up. He walked from the rear of the church to the front at the altar and stood there. The congregation went wild, all except our mother. She simply sat as if to say it was just a matter of time. Yeah, 40 years!

From that point on our father never missed a Sunday coming to church and he had a reserved spot in the parking lot for his motorcycle. I'm surprised that the attendant didn't have a sign on his spot that read, "Reserved for the Pastor's Father!"

Growing Pains

My parents owned and operated the local dry cleaners in our neighborhood from 1953 to 1963. I must have been nine or ten when I learned to write up the cleaning receipts for the customers and tag the clothes. It was wonderful having my parents at home, yet at work and just three stairs away working in the cleaners. It was fun writing receipts after completing my homework, especially on the days I wasn't home in bed suffering from asthma attacks.

I remember a pot similar to a tea kettle that my mother would connect near my bed. Steam would flow from it as it was one of the few things that would help me to breathe. There were days that I breathed so hard that my entire body would move up and down, from my feet to my head. Anything people told my mother to try, she would, like boil banana peels, boil Vick's vapor rub, put hot towels on my chest, anything to help her baby girl breathe.

Being the believer that she was, my mother kept me in as many prayer lines that were called at church and she always believed that I would be healed. I suffered from age six until around twelve, but I can't remember exactly when I was healed. I just remember the attacks stopped. The attacks would cause me to miss school at least two weeks a month. Later in high school when the teachers would mention historical events, I had no idea what they would be talking about, so I would ask my friends about it and they would ask, "Where were you when we were studying this in elementary school and junior high?" My response would be, "At home coloring in my coloring books and reading Archie comics, hoping to be able to take my next breath." Those were the two things that I enjoyed most that kept me busy for hours while my parents worked in the cleaners.

I enjoyed singing but that was out of the question prior to the 6th grade. I simply wanted to breathe. During the 6th grade my teacher heard me singing one day as I passed her and she suggested that I join the school choir. That seemed like a good idea because I had started to sing in the children's choir at church. No one had any idea that I would one day become a professional singer and record with the likes of Stevie Wonder and work in the industry as a studio contractor.

My Classmates

There was a Chinese family that owned and operated the local corner grocery store. They lived on the premises of their business just like we did. During the weeks I wasn't home fighting asthma, their daughter Kim, my other three friends, Karla, Pecola, Eleta and I often walked to school together. We were classmates in the same second grade class.

One morning, when Mr. Frazier, one of the alcoholics in our community went to the store, for the first time ever, it wasn't open. He was retired and his wife would issue him a weekly allowance. By the end of each week all of his money would have been spent on drinks, so he would volunteer to go to the corner store for the neighbors to purchase any needed staples, like milk, bread, eggs, etc. His wife had assured the grocery store owners that she would pay for any food items that he requested at the end of each month. The neighbors would send him to the store, just like he was a seven or eight year old. Upon his return with the items they would pay him with cash. But he was charging the items to his wife's bill and using the cash from the neighbors to purchase his spirits. He was an alcoholic yes, dummy no. This went on for months before his wife figured out what he was actually accomplishing at her expense.

Lets get back to the Chinese family. Wanting his morning drink, Mr. Frazier immediately walked to the rear of the property but noticed that there were no signs of anyone being awake. He began to bang on the windows and doors, finally rousing up Kim's parents, and her grandmother, who was responsible for washing the vegetables at the store. I can't remember going into the store without seeing her lightly spraying the vegetables in the bins. She rarely spoke, just nodded her head to gesture a hello.

Then their two sons staggered out of the store. One was a pre-teen and the older was probably about 14-years-old at the time. Everyone was out of the house, except Kim. Realizing that she wasn't outdoors, her father rushed back in, but not soon enough. Kim was gone. She had passed away in her sleep due to gas escaping from their stove. I must have been 7-years-old. It was tragic and devastating.

When the local newspaper printed the story, I remember my mother asking me to take the article to our teacher for her to read to the class. Having to sit through class that day and listen to the teacher read the article aloud was one of the hardest things I had to endure up to that point in my life. It was worse than the asthma attacks. I believe that was the day I became acquainted with God. I remember asking Him to help me make it through that particular day. I had heard my mother talk about how He was always close by and that we could count on Him, but I hadn't been healed and hadn't really been in a position to know Him for myself. Yes, I attended Sunday school, actually every week but nothing was really real to me. I would sit and doubt the stories that were being taught by the teachers and pastor, but that day in school things changed for me. My parents were nowhere near to comfort me. I knew at that point that there was something great carrying me. My friend was gone and I would never see her again.

The paper heralded Mr. Frazier as a hero. If he had not gone for his drink they may have all died.

The Shooting

By the time I was ending junior high school; my parents had closed the cleaners and rented out the storefronts, one to a gentleman who repaired televisions and the other to a beautician who had two other women who rented booths from her. Mrs. Idle was a very sweet lady and one who meant business all the way. She had three children who were five, eight and twelve years old. Her twelve year old son was her business partner and would care for his younger siblings as his mother worked. He would come to the salon, with his siblings in both hands, collect the money she had earned by mid day, take it to the bank, make deposits, return home and begin dinner for her.

One day as Mrs. Idle dressed my mother's hair, I overheard her tell my mother that her husband would not work to support their family. I would accompany my mother to the salon, watching every move Mrs. Idle made, wanting someday to become a beautician. By the way, I did work in that very salon as co-owner and beautician

Ruthell Cook Price

for ten years along with my mother after completing high school and beauty college in 1969.

This particular day was different. Mrs. Idle began to pour her heart out to my mother, one who often counseled people who were in despair. She began to share the ups and downs of her marriage and said how she pondered if she should separate from Mr. Idle.

As a young child, I sat and listened as they talked, never saying a word, knowing that wouldn't be the thing to do when adults were talking, not even to ask if I could go to the restroom. I can't remember the advice my mother offered Mrs. Idle that day, if any. Sometimes she would just listen, but several weeks later she told my mother that she and her children had moved out of the house.

Soon after, she informed my mother that she had moved away, tragedy struck our community once again. Early one morning we heard Mrs. Idle opening the salon's iron barred door and the clanking of the bars as she pushed the "V" shaped bars together. We heard her enter the salon each morning, preparing for her clients, but this day was different. She never set foot inside. As she pushed the rod iron bars back we heard a shotgun blast ring out. My mother and I were in the kitchen preparing breakfast. My brothers were asleep and my father was in the backyard piddling around in the garage, as he so often did. The blast was so loud and at that very moment everything seemed to move in slow motion for me. My mother immediately began to scream, "Mr. Idle just shot Mrs. Idle." She just knew it.

My brothers jumped up out of bed. The younger one, Donald, jumped into his jeans as fast as he could. Being the high school track star that he was ran toward the front door. My mother yelled, "No, no, he may still be there." But Donald ran out the front door, never pausing, around to the boulevard, with my brother and father close behind him. They found Mrs. Idle lying on the sidewalk in front of the salon with a shotgun wound to her stomach. My brother ran to her, and kneeling he placed her head in his lap. He immediately asked, "Who shot you, Mrs. Idle?" She was able to respond and said, "My husband. Donald, don't let him get away." The ambulance came shortly thereafter, but she passed away en-route to the hospital. Her husband was caught and arrested two blocks north of the salon, hiding in the Helm's Bakery parking lot. My brother never had to testify. Mr. Idle admitted to the crime as soon as the officers arrived and arrested him. He was still holding the weapon.

It was an awful day. The neighbors often gathered to discuss the tragedy. We heard later that Mr. Idle was sentenced to many years in prison and we never saw him again. The oldest son remained a supporting caretaker of his siblings along with a distant relative as their surrogate mother. The sound of the shotgun still remains with me. I can only imagine what my brothers and father saw that day.

During the 9th grade and throughout high school I sang. Brenda Holloway, a recording artist with Motown, who recorded "Every Little Bit Hurts," had a younger sister named Patrice. She and I became good friends at Drew Junior High. We would sing during and after school while riding home together. Her mother picked us up and we would sing, harmonizing all the way home, singing runs that was really very good for twelve year olds. Her mother would tell us that we weren't sounding very good but we ignored her and kept singing and laughing as we attempted to mimic the artists with the latest hit record.

High school was good. No tragedies, no asthma, just a lot of singing. Thank goodness! I maintained a friendship with several friends from Junior High. Two of them, Brenda Peppars and Brenda Piggee, became singing partners with me. We were called "The Cream of the Crop," and sang professionally as background for Mel Lastie and Harold Battiste, both gifted musicians from New Orleans. My brother Donald was the keyboardist.

There were others, bringing our buddy group to a total of nine. The group included Brenda, Brenda and

Brenda, (one of the Brenda's attended Washington High) and all of the rest of us attended Fremont High: Donna, Sharon, Karla, Katherine, Mamie and I. I can't leave out Roy, our high school class president and soon to be my brother-in-law. Yep, I married his older brother, Fred. Roy was the person who helped me through junior and senior high school math classes while I helped him get through the English classes. It's something how he became the CPA and now 46 years later I'm writing. Forty-six years of camaraderie, smiles and tears.

CHAPTER TWO

HUSBANDS

The Champ Picks Up the Tab

Tribute to Joe Louis "The Champ"

My first husband and I met in high school. When I was a freshman, he was a senior and one of my best friend's older brother. He was one of the star football and baseball players during his junior and senior years and best friend to Willie Crawford, who later went on to play pro baseball with the Los Angeles Dodgers.

We dated for two years and he was one of the few guys my parents trusted. We attended most musical concerts that featured such artists as James Brown, The Temptations, Four Tops, Marvin Gaye and many others. We rarely missed any of these events as we arrived in his bright and loud GTO. Often we would lead approximately 12-15 cars to parks for holiday picnics, beach outings and local parties. We just had plain fun in our late teens to early twenties without any incidents, such as gang violence, car accidents, etc.

In 1967 he was drafted into the U.S. Army and served in Viet Nam for two years. While he was there, it was prom time for our high school. And there I was without a date, being true blue to my sweetheart in Viet Nam.

I was asked by the senior counselors if I would sing at the prom, I guess (instead of them hiring a pro). I agreed after asking my brother if he would bring his singing group along to sing background for me and to open the show. He agreed and so did I.

It was a great night for all. Later I was asked if I would consider coming back to The Grove to sing again. Yes, The Ambassador Hotel/The Coconut Grove in Los Angeles, a very popular, upscale hotel lounge and dinner spot primarily for adults only, and yes, the same place where Senator Bobby Kennedy was later assassinated. My mother wasn't having it, being the Christian and wanting me to become as devoted as she was.

My sweetheart returned in 1970, after completing his military term. We became engaged soon after his return. I was attending junior college at the time and working as a cosmetologist in my salon. My salon was located on a boulevard that's now considered in South Central, Los Angeles. At the time it was simply called the east side of Los Angeles.

My mother and I mapped out a plan that would take one year to complete for the preparation of my wedding. Every Monday, which was our off day, we would meet with someone connected to this big event, such as the baker. No one was called a cake designer at the time. At least no one on the east side knew anyone who had that title. We met with the wedding coordinator of the church, who was probably the church secretary at the time, and with the dressmaker for the bridesmaids dresses. I ended up purchasing the first gown I tried on from a bridal shop in Westchester, Calif. That was easy. We didn't have much money, actually any money, to plan such an event, but people were kind and very supportive of the ideas I had for my special day.

I remember meeting with the estate coordinator of the Winfandel House on Adams to plan my reception, completing the paper work and signing their register. I found out later that someone else had booked a reception on the very same day, which would have conflicted with my time at the facility. The coordinator had failed to turn the page in the calendar booklet to check to see if someone else was scheduled for the room on that day. However it all worked out okay. The other family was contacted and agreed to move their reception up one hour and we moved mine back one hour so the two parties would not clash. We were all happy that both receptions went off without a hitch.

When we went to a Black-owned bakery, actually a Black Muslim-owned and operated one, my mother and I explained exactly what we wanted. I wanted a fountain cake so badly and when we explained it to the gentleman he said that he was sorry but didn't have access to fountains for cakes. I was crushed but because he was so kind and his prices so reasonable, we agreed to have him prepare a cake that would not require the fountain that I desired so much.

On the day before my wedding the bakery contacted my mother to say they had located a fountain and that I would have my fountain wedding cake. I was so happy about that phone call that I just jumped and shouted.

On the morning of the wedding, my father decided to drink himself into a drunken state. There were just too many people running around for him. So he decided to get drunk and go to bed. About two hours before we had to leave for the church, we tried to wake up my dad. Unable to do so, we called and asked my uncle to walk me down the aisle. He refused, stating that he felt he just couldn't, and he would be entirely too nervous. So it was decided that my oldest brother would walk me as my younger brother would be singing and driving our limo, borrowed from one of his friends.

My dad walked out of his bedroom fully dressed, shining from head to toe in his best suit approximately twenty minutes before leaving for the church. I'm so grateful it was black. Not being a church goer like our mother, he had two suits—one black and one gold— the gold one was of the Cab Calloway look. If he had insisted on wearing the gold suit, I do believe I would not have gotten married that day.

We all arrived at the church on time with me running up to the loft of the church, which was the pastor's office, to slip into my dress. As I peeped out of the small window in his office, I could see people arriving in their cars, coming from the east, west, north and south. I had attended this church, which was probably considered a mega church in the 70s, my entire life and had served in all youth groups and activities. I had sung with the children's choir, teen choir and in my late teens joined the adult choir. I would rehearse the lead on the phone with our minister of music while doing hair in my salon.

I can remember the pastor calling on me to sing one of his favorite songs, "Jesus Be A Fence All Around Me." For the pastor to call on you, it was a big thing!

As people continued to arrive, the ushers pushed back the accordion partitions so people could sit in the overflow section of the church and some in the choir loft. There were over three hundred people in attendance.

I had requested that all family members wear white. My six bridesmaids wore short white chiffon dresses with white headpieces, resembling the "Flying Nun's" (the TV show) head dress, and they were simply unique and pretty. The groomsmen wore black tuxedos with white accessories and the groom wore a white jacket and black pants. I wore a long, fitted, white lace gown and had a very long veil coming out of the top of a pillbox-styled hat. My dress and the bridesmaids dresses had short puffed sleeves, which was very unique for wedding attire at the time.

As the guest arrived, to their delight, they received printed programs from the ushers, a first for our church. With my ringbearer Tony, two flower girls—Tranesha and Joy, and trainbearer Chisa, everything went quite well during the wedding. There were doubts, because of the slight scuffle at the wedding rehearsal between the two flower girls. One decided to throw flowers from the other's basket.

Our limousine led the way followed by a caravan of very nice cars containing the wedding party. All of the cars had white stuffed doves on the antennas with white streamers fluttering in the wind during the drive. It was a beautiful sight to see as we approached the Wilfandel House for the reception. We were praying all the way there after staying at the church as long as possible, taking photo after photo, actually stalling for time. Upon our arrival, the other party was already gone and the place was clean and cleared for us.

My new husband and I left the reception, rushing home to change clothes and were driven to the airport to catch our flight to Las Vegas, Nevada. We had made reservations at Caesar's Palace for our honeymoon.

Our seats on the plane were near the wings and I was so excited about everything. I kept looking down the aisle to see who was boarding. To my surprise, the now retired heavyweight boxing champ Joe Louis, accompanied by a younger White gentleman entered the plane. I recognized him from watching his fights along with my dad on television as a young child. As they walked closer, I hunched my new husband and said, "Look it's Joe Louis, the Heavyweight Boxing Champion." But he had already sat down at his assigned seat in front of ours. So my husband thought I was mistaken. He never saw Mr. Louis' face but I continued to tell him that I was sure it was him.

As soon as the plane landed, I asked my husband if we could rush so that we could pass Mr. Louis while he was still in his seat. That way he could see that it was really him. He agreed and we hurried toward the front of the plane, almost pushing the people that were in front of us. I had to prove to my husband that it was actually him, The Champ. As we approached his seat, I stopped, so sure that it was him and said, "Hello Mr. Louis, how are you?" He was so nice. He smiled and said hello and proceeded to ask about our visit to Vegas. We were 21 and 24 years old at the time so I guess he thought we may have been even younger. I explained that we were on our honeymoon. My husband was star struck as I kept talking. The Champ congratulated us and we parted.

We flagged down a taxi cab and arrived at Caesar's Palace on the Strip. As we approached the front entrance to the hotel, we saw several cabs arriving, and one was carrying Mr. Louis and the gentleman who accompanied him on the plane.

Greeting each other once again, Mr. Louis was shocked to learn that we would be staying at Caesar's Palace. We had no idea that he had been hired as a host to greet the guest at Caesar's. He walked with us to the front reservation desk then asked the receptionist for our booking information. The young man handed him an envelope, which appeared to be a reservation packet. After a conversation with the receptionist that we could not hear, Mr. Louis turned to us and said good bye and he hoped that we will enjoy our stay at The Palace. At that point I felt as though we had become good friends.

My husband and I checked in and were handed the keys to our room. We were escorted to the closest elevator by the valet who had placed our luggage on his cart. He had truly been taught to be kind, hoping to receive a hefty tip I'm sure. As he opened the door to our room, we stepped in and said "Oh no, there's been a mistake. This is not the room we requested." We knew immediately that we could not afford the room we were standing in. It was lavishly furnished with a step up into the bedroom area, with a bench at the foot of the king size bed that was the actual length of the bed. Oops, wrong room!

We rushed back down to the front lobby with the young valet following with our luggage neatly stacked on his cart. We went directly to the gentleman who had originally registered us to explain that a mistake had been made with our room.

He remembered us and smiled and said "No sir (to my husband), there hasn't been a mistake. Mr. Louis upgraded your room. He will pay the additional cost of your room throughout your stay." He went on to say, "In your package, you will receive fruit and drinks in your room and two passes to one of the shows in our hotel, all compliments of Mr. Louis." Joe Louis was our Muhammad Ali in the 60s. What a champion athlete.

We could not believe what we were hearing. We went back to the elevator, anxious to get back to tour our suite along with the valet and his luggage cart. Oh my Lord! What a place. It had a very large living room as you open the door to the suite, with two or three steps leading to the bedroom area and of course a completely marbled bathroom.

The next day about mid afternoon, there was a knock on the door of our suite, then a voice saying "housekeeper." When my husband opened the door there was a middle-aged Black lady with a very pretty smile, who entered offering to clean our room. She was so surprised to see a young Black couple in such a luxurious room. As soon as my husband walked a few steps away from her, she softly asked me, "Is your husband a baseball player?" I smiled and said no. My husband did look like a professional baseball player and coincidently was earlier offered a minor league contract. Apparently only the pros had access to that floor at the Palace.

It was like OK we are dead and stopped off in Vegas en-route to heaven and Mr. Louis was our assigned angel. It was just too much excitement for one day, and yes, we tipped the valet and mailed a very nice thank you letter back to "The Champ" at his beautiful Palace!

Church Meeting

My husband and I met at church, Sunday, January 1984. At the conclusion of the morning worship service, my brother, the pastor asked the question, "Is there anyone present today that desires to make this your church home?" That particular Sunday more people wanted to become members of the church than any other Sunday that I can recall from 1976 to 1984. I counted 13 people coming forward to give their names and accept Christ into their lives.

Our procedure was to walk the new candidates out of the church and to issue application forms to them to be completed and returned to the church clerk. That particular Sunday the candidates were various ages, from pre-teens to adult.

That evening, several of the new members returned to the church for service. Among them was a gentleman who was to become my second husband. He was neatly dressed, and well groomed. Prior to departing from the church sanctuary one of the deacons walked him over to introduce him to me. He said, "I want you to meet our church administrator and pastor's sister." I nodded and said, "Yes, we met this morning." He told me later that I basically ignored him that evening.

The following Sunday he returned and sat in the very rear of the church. During the offertory service, he reached to pull an envelope from the pew in front of his seat but pulled one that had a child's handwriting and numbers on it that appeared to be a phone number. It happened to be my home phone number. It was written by Channing, my five year old son. He was the children's church drummer at the time. Yep, age five. He was so small that my nephew Lloyd Michael, the sanctuary drummer, would pick him up and sit him in his lap to allow him to reach the drums as he worked the foot pedal for the bass. Channing now 32-years old, still laughs and says people came to church to watch him play drums.

Following service that evening, the new member approached me to show me the envelope. Someone had told him that the little drummer's name was Channing and that he was my son. He handed me the envelope and asked if that was my phone number on it. I nodded and said yes. He politely took the envelope out of my hand and asked if he could call me. Again I nodded and said yes.

The same deacon came back to me a week later and said it would be nice if the three of us would have lunch together and how important it was to show the new members love. I agreed. We were to meet at my job on Wednesday and have lunch together. The new member showed up at my job and on time. As he approached the entry way, my phone rang…it was the deacon calling to say he couldn't make the luncheon date. At that point I knew I had been set up by him. Mr. New Member was so pleased to have me all to himself.

We had lunch. It was nice. Later I sent a note of thanks…I really believe that did it. The second date was slated and he was to pick me up following work and drive me to Stevie Wonder's recording studio for a scheduled session. I was singing at that time with the gospel group, "Harvest" and Stevie had contracted us for a background session coordinated by my friend Karla. En-route home from the session, Kenneth, Mr. New Member asked me to marry him and I did two months later.

We purchased a home and moved my parents in with us. My Mother had developed Parkinson and Alzheimer's disease and my Father had recently completed chemo treatments.

After several months of marriage, Kenneth left the city without any notice, under duress from the legal system. Everything changed, small things, big things. It was just hard to focus. Going to the supermarket became a difficult task, even though it was something I enjoyed prior to his departure. Remembering to purchase Ensure for my mother, diapers and baby food for my newborn and Gatorade for my teenager became a major task. This time in my life reminded me of the movie ET, the scene when the mother would walk pass ET in the house and never noticed him.

For the next seven years, I never heard from my husband at all. I never knew where he lived, or if he was even alive. Periodically I would become so depressed that I would phone his family members asking of his whereabouts or if he was alive. But they rarely had any information to offer.

I would only speak well of Kenneth to our son and pray for both of them. My little boy would listen intently to what any and everyone had to say about his father. Everyone always made sure it was positive because he really was a good person, just caught in a destructive vice.

One day at church Carolynn, one of the members of the singing group I was in began to speak about my husband and my son asked, "Do you know my father?" Her response was, "Sure, he is a very nice man." He offered her a tiny smile.

Several months passed and one day his Sunday school teacher, Mrs. Bettie Mullin phoned me to say, "Your son came to me today following class to ask me to pray with him that his father would return. It blew me away. I did not know that he wanted so desperately to know him. He was now 7-years-old, so uncles and friends could no longer stand in for his dad. She informed me that the two of them prayed together after all the children filed out of the classroom that Sunday.

After seven years of silence, and three weeks after my son's prayer, he met his father. God answers children's prayers as well as adults.

See "Kodak Moment" for Part II.

Hot and Sweaty, In Clear View

My son Channing returned home from a stint on Broadway, where he was a featured principle dancer in "Riverdance, The Broadway Show." After one day at home he seemed to be quite bored. I asked, "What would you be doing if you were still in New York?" "Mom I had a routine. I would go to the gym, then practice drums in a nearby studio, home to rest for the show, leave for the show at approx 5:00 p.m., stop at Starbucks for coffee, and jump on a train en-route to the theatre for the 8:00 p.m. curtain call," was his reply.

Immediately it occurred to me to ask him to accompany me on a short trip. I drove to the closest Bally Total Fitness Center, located in the City of Hawthorne and went directly to the business office to ask about enrollment for him. The manager was such a salesman. He quickly asked, "Well what about you mom?" I thought, "What was he trying to say, even though I knew I needed a lot of fitness work." But within twenty minutes both Channing and I were signed up for a two year program.

We would go to the gym together on the average twice a week. After about the third week, I decided to venture out and experience the sauna. There happened to be only one gentleman in there.

We were both seated facing the window to the open gymnasium, where we could see practically everyone. We were on the same row of the bleacher, not looking at one another nor saying a word. A least I thought he hadn't looked in my direction. But after about 10 minutes of silence, he said, "I've seen you before, may I ask what you do?"

I thought to myself "Sure you've seen me, what a lame excuse to talk." I wanted no parts of this conversation, especially after trying to rekindle a second marriage that had been out of commission for seven years. I had no idea that the man who just said to me, "I've seen you before," would be my third husband. I finally stopped talking to myself and tried to hold a decent conversation. I explained that I was in the banking industry and had been for many years. He proceeded to name the banks that serviced his accounts. Having never worked for any of them, at that point, I found the conversation to be amusing. He left the spa trying to figure out where he had seen me before, and I left thinking he was making it all up.

That particular day, I had gone to the gym with my girlfriend Gerie. After we got dressed and met in the lobby of the gym, I told her that I had met a guy in the spa, who actually appeared to be very nice, but I didn't feel as though I had been cordial to him. She suggested that we wait for him outside so I could start over. I agreed thinking yeah, something is different about this one. It was a Saturday and the gym was closing at 8:00 p.m. We waited for quite a while, thinking, well he has to eventually come out and when he did, he was fully dressed in motorcycle gear, carrying his helmet.

My immediate thought was, Okay, let's go, he's a member of the Hell's Angels. In my mind, anyone riding a motorcycle was a Hell's Angel. Gerie said, "No, let's talk to him." As he walked to his bike, I beckoned for him to come to my car. He casually walked over, unable to clearly see me in the driver's seat and not knowing who Gerie was. But as he got closer and leaned over, he was able to see that it was me, the mean lady from the spa.

I smiled and said, "I never asked you your name." He replied, "Mark Price." "It was nice meeting you and hope to see you again. This is my friend, Gerie," I said. He smiled and shook Gerie's hand. As I put the car in reverse to leave, I remembered that the next day was Father's Day and said, "Happy Father's Day tomorrow. You are a father aren't you?" He replied, "Yes" and gave us a big smile. I drove away thinking well, that was nice, but I'll never see him again.

I actually thought of him off and on all week. Mark Price, nice name, nice guy. I began to think back on the conversation we had in the sauna. Computer troubleshooter who frequents the gym prior to work. There was something drawing me to him...his calmness, his voice, had a job, maybe a combination of all three. But the bike concerned me. I couldn't see myself having anything to do with a man who rode a bike! I was way too conservative, or scary, for that.

About mid-week I went to visit my brother, the pastor, and his wife. I began to talk about the gentleman I had met in the gym. I mentioned that his name was Mark and that mine was Ruth, as if he didn't know both names were biblical. My brother said, "Please don't go there, and let me say this, if you see him again and he asks you out to dinner, don't plan your wedding or name your children while having your first meal with him. Some men just want to have dinner. They would rather not eat alone all the time." I thought that was reasonable and agreed as I laughed about what he had just said.

One week after I met Mark, I went back to the gym, hoping to run into him again. It was on the following Saturday at the very same time I happened to be there the previous week. But no Mark. Would you believe it? I ran into my ex-husband instead. Yep, husband number two! I could not believe it. He actually accused me of coming to that particular gym looking for him. I couldn't speak, I was so disgusted. I finally regrouped, stepped into the sauna and had a few words with him prior to leaving. I left the gym that night saddened but halfway to my car I broke out into laughter, thinking how bad my luck was. I had been looking for and anticipated seeing Mark again but ran into number two!

Channing and I continued our twice a week routine the following week. On our second visit, I was starting my workout, stretching and up walks Mark. We said hello and continued our workout together. Before departing that day we agreed that we would exercise on the same days of the week and meet in the sauna, which would give us more time to talk. We began to meet regularly.

One day in the sauna he mentioned dinner. I didn't push it because I didn't feel quite ready for dinner yet. At that point he was really trying to feel me out. I remember bringing him a bottle of water because he had previously mentioned that he always forgot to bring some. He was so impressed that I thought to bring him a bottle of water. I thought, Wow, if a bottle of water impressed him, this is not going to be hard at all.

I began to write notes to Mark and leave them on his bike or with the parking attendant who actually became our middle person and enjoyed watching him read the notes prior to spinning off on his motorcycle. Mark would call me upon his arrival to work to thank me for the notes. I would write things like, enjoyed the gym today, let's talk soon, thanks for the fitness lesson today, etc. He was an avid fitness person and had been for years. He taught me how to use most of the equipment. It was his patience and the way he spoke to me that drew me closer and closer each week.

One day he came to visit and I asked if he would ride with me to a store in Westchester. He replied, "Yes, what store?" I said, "Trader Joe's." That's when it hit him. He loudly and excitedly said, "That's where I first saw you. Several weeks ago, my brother Michael and my son Jonathan and I stopped at Trader Joe's in Westchester. You were in the store in line behind me. I happened to turn around and spotted you and thought, she's attractive. I went to my car where my brother and son were waiting. I deliberately stalled hoping you would come out soon. I told my brother I wanted him to see a lady who was in the line behind me. We waited until you walked out and you walked right past us, never looking in our direction. My brother said, 'Yea man.'"

After meeting his brother a short time later and confirming that they had seen me at the store, I thought he's truthful and it wasn't a come-on line after all. I began to thank God for Traders Joe's and Bally's Total Fitness. We got married fourteen months later.

CHAPTER THREE

MY SONS

Mickey Mouse Is Black

When my son, Channing turned five years old, I decided to try my hand at getting him into modeling and show business. One of his first auditions was for a photo shoot, advertising a new children's clothing line for Disney.

The audition site was Griffith Park in Los Angeles. I talked to him all the way to the park, assuring him that he could land this job if he continued to smile and act like a nice little boy. He was so full of energy and appeared to be ready for anything once we pulled into the parking area.

Upon our arrival, there was a small yellow school bus parked near the trailer where he would be interviewed. Several people were at the site as well, parents with children, a Black man about the age of 35, and several young people who appeared to be assistants to the three people who interviewed the children.

My son was called into the trailer shortly after our arrival. When he walked out, a gentleman accompanied him who walked over to me and asked if I would allow him to be the star of the photo shoot. I asked him what being the star required. He explained that my son would be the child to stand in front of the bus with several of the Disney characters. All of the other children were going to be in the bus which was parked nearby.

The photo shoot was to take place the same day, in fact within minutes. My son was escorted into a trailer to change into one of the outfits that would be introduced and sold as part of Disney's new fall clothing line for elementary school-age children.

Within minutes the children who were selected were asked to board the parked bus, stick their heads out of the windows, smile and wave, as the Black gentleman sat in the driver's seat. It was really going to be a cute ad.

A few moments later, Channing walked out of the trailer dressed in new clothes, leading the way for Mickey Mouse, Pluto and Donald Duck. He was all teeth, and very proud to be the one selected to stand outside of the bus with the Disney characters.

The shoot was quite successful. The photographer and producers were pleased and it was time to go back to the trailer and put his clothes back on. He insisted that he could do it alone. So I waited nearby.

It wasn't very long before Channing came out of the trailer, ready to head home. We walked to our car, and began to drive home. But I noticed that he was very quiet.

I thought that he must have been tired. Normally he was a chatter box, so I wondered if everything was okay.

I broke the silence by asking if it was fun meeting the Disney characters. He looked at me with an expression I hadn't seen before that moment and said, "Mom, Mickey Mouse is Black." It was a look of, Wow, he's Black.

"Really Channing?" I asked. "Yes mom he is Black," he replied.

I wondered why on earth he would think that. Was it something Mickey said? I knew the characters weren't allowed to speak a word to any children while in costume but for him to think that Mickey Mouse was Black, that was puzzling to me.

"Did he tell you he was Black or how do you know he's Black?" I asked. "I was standing very close to him mom and saw his neck," he replied.

He didn't speak another word all the way home. I thought about our day that evening. How motivating it must have been for a five year old Black child to discover that a Black person was portraying the most popular theme park character in the whole world.

Last Name

My son Channing was excited about starting pre-school. I was working full time and my mother was his sitter. She drove him up to the school twice to allow him to watch the children on the playground. They would sit in the car and she asked him questions like, "You understand that you cannot wet your pants?" and "you will have to tell your teacher that you have to go to the bathroom, right?" "You will have to obey your teacher at all times okay?" He had the right answer for each of her questions. He wanted to attend school so badly.

The first day of school went well. He enjoyed every minute of his day and explained to his grandmother, Honey, he now had lots of friends and they played games together indoors and on the playground. He was so happy.

On the second day of school his teacher requested that everyone learn the first and last name of the person sitting next to them. My mother picked him up at the usual time of 1:00 p.m. and as she drove to the grocery store she began to ask him about his day. He explained that he had to remember his classmate's first and last name. His assigned person's name was Jeffrey Jones.

As they walked into the grocery store, Honey asked him to assist her with the shopping. She placed him in the child's section of the cart and began her shopping by placing a jar of dip into the basket, later picking up a large bag of Ruffles potato chips. Channing had never had dip before and wondered what was in the jar. He noticed the bag of chips and asked if he could have some in the car on the way home. She responded yes.

She later asked him to hold on to two smaller unbreakable items, giving him something to do. He held the boxed toothpaste and a small package of napkins, assisting Grandmom Honey with pride. He later explained to me how he helped Honey with shopping by holding toothpaste and napkins.

After they completed the check out, she placed him in the car and handed him the bag of potato chips, assuring him that he was going to get some chips while riding home. As she got into the car he noticed that she was holding the jar that was in the basket earlier. Before starting the engine, she opened the bag of chips and handed him a few. Then she unscrewed the jar and dipped one of her chips into it. He watched her intensely then asked what was in the jar. "Dip," she answered. Totally unaware of what dip was, he asked, "What's Dip's last name?"

Honey's Watchman

In 1988, my husband and I were blessed to purchase a home large enough to accommodate my parents, he and I and my 10-year-old son, Channing.

My father was a cancer patient and mother had begun to develop Parkinson's Disease, followed by showing signs of Alzheimer in 1991. Prior to moving them from their home of 33 years, I would cook weekly and deliver meals to last for several days at a time, only to return and find that the meals had not been touched.

My brothers and I consulted with their medical doctors and were simply told that in order for them to live a while longer, they needed to live with one of us. I was their only daughter. So I took on the responsibility after months of much prayer and petitioning God to grant me the means to purchase a larger home and the strength to care for them.

My father passed away one year after we moved together. After their 51 years of marriage, I felt the pain and grief would have been too much for my mother to bear alone each day. I could not afford a sitter, so without my mother's knowledge, I asked my 11-year-old son if he would come home on his lunch hour each day to check on my mom "Honey." It was a nickname she had selected earlier for her grands to call her. She didn't quite like the Grandmother title. Channing readily agreed, remembering how much fun they had together throughout the years.

I contacted his school explaining the situation and they agreed to allow him to leave campus for lunch each day. It was so stressful for me to leave her each day having to drive 35 miles to work.

I went to her and explained that Channing didn't care for the food at school and how grateful he and I would be if she would prepare his lunch each day. She agreed. I felt that would take my father's death off her mind, at least temporarily while he was home. He would leave school at 11:45 a.m. and arrive home at 11:52. She would constantly watch the clock to make sure that his lunch would be prepared upon his arrival.

Each night he and I would discuss his time at home with her. He told me things like, "The soup was warm enough today," and "The sandwich was cut in quarters like I like it." Prior to his departure to return to school, and without her knowledge, he would check the stove, oven, heaters and back door to make sure our home was safe.

Several weeks passed and one day, Honey said to me, "You know Channing is very different from most children." I asked her to explain. She said "Before he arrives each day for lunch, I walk outside to see if I can see him approaching and you know, he's the only child that comes home for lunch on this block. You would think that he would want to stay at school and have lunch and play with the other children." I simply smiled and said, "Mother he really enjoys coming home and spending that time with you."

After about four months of spending their lunch time together she came to me and said, "You know I'd like to rest more during the day and I can't with Channing coming home for lunch everyday." That was the point where I felt her grief had somewhat subsided and I could release Honey's watchman.

Key's Please

I decided to attend a church conference in Oklahoma with friends Constance and Linda, and asked if one of the mothers of our church, Mary Blackmon, Constance's mother, would stay with my four year old son Lladon, fifteen and a half years old son Channing, and my ailing mother. She agreed and I was thankful for the break.

As I prepared to depart, excited about the trip which was so needed, I called a meeting with everyone, Mrs. Blackmon, my mother, and sons. I left contact information with them, hotel, phone numbers, etc. and explained to the boys that Mrs. Blackmon was in charge and they were to be obedient at all times.

I was picked up and driven to the airport, leaving my car in the garage and keys with Mrs. Blackmon. I left home on a Wednesday morning and was scheduled to return late evening that following Saturday. Upon my arrival to my destination, I phoned home to check on everyone and things were fine.

From Wednesday evening to Friday morning, I enjoyed the conference and the company of my friends.

Saturday morning, upon arrival to the airport I phoned home again to let everyone know that I was about to board a plane home. As I began asking Mrs. Blackmon about everyone, I could distinctly hear that something had gone very wrong. I asked her if everything was okay. She said, "Yes," but with hesitation.

Fear became an imposition on my mind. All the way home I wondered what would I face upon arrival. It happened to be the worse flight I had ever experienced. We flew through a thunder storm. The windows were covered with rain and the one friend who was traveling back to L.A. with me had a fear of flying. She was a nervous wreck! Every time we would hit an air pocket she would yell, squeeze my hand tightly and ask if I was praying. Of course I was, praying that she would leave me alone! We finally landed after much turbulence and prayer, but the fear of going home was worse than what I had experienced on the flight home.

As the cab pulled into my driveway, Mrs. Blackmon walked outside of the house to meet me. I could tell it was not going to be a welcome greeting but one that would be unpleasant. She looked like she had been through something very uncomfortable.

As she approached, she said, "I need to talk to you." My heart began to race. I could not imagine what she was about to say to me. I pulled my luggage up onto the front porch and into the house as slowly as possible thinking what could have possibly happened.

We sat down and she began to talk. She said, "About 7:00 p.m. Friday night, I opened the garage door to take some trash out and your new Cadillac was gone, not there, removed, missing. I immediately developed a sweaty forehead and my body became limp."

She said she immediately rushed to my son Channing's bedroom, with trash still in hand, to ask if he had any idea what happened to my car. Unable to find him anywhere in the house, she immediately rushed to her room to look for my keys. I had left them with her in the event she needed to move the car while I was away. The keys were nowhere to be found.

She rushed to my neighbors home, one of Channing's school mates, to asked if he knew where Channing could possibly be and if he knew whether he took my car. Nathan said, "Yes, I overheard him tell some of our friends that he would meet them at a skating party at a rink in Downey." She yelled, "Downey!"

Downey was 18 miles from Inglewood. Wondering if he took the freeway made matters worse. So she rushed back home and phoned my brother to tell him of the theft and who the thief was! His response was, "When he returns, and I pray that he will in one piece, take the keys immediately and call me."

Channing returned home safely at approximately 9:00 p.m. to the greeting from Mrs. Blackmon of KEYS, PLEASE! He had no driver's license, no learner's permit to drive and of course no insurance to cover him. I only had insurance covering legitimate adult drivers, not thieves. I didn't know he could drive. I hadn't taught him nor his father. I had recently purchased the car and was so thankful to finally have a new one.

When she finished telling me about her Friday escapade, I called both boys in—Channing to lecture and Lladon to hear every word I had to say, hoping that he wouldn't do the same when he turned 15 or 16. I was drained and weak simply thinking of what could have happened, his death, someone else's death or injury, followed by my mental breakdown. I could only imagine how she felt actually experiencing all of it.

I began to lecture. I went on forever, asking questions like, "Did you go alone?" "Did you take the freeway?" Tired from the start, I couldn't bear to hear myself any longer. I ended by asking, "Do you guys realize how much I love you both?"

They nodded and softly said, "Yes." I finally ended the lecture and dismissed them both from the room. Before leaving, my youngest, Lladon, age 4-1/2 asked, "Mommie may I say something before I leave?" I responded, "Yes." His "say something" was, "Mommie, at least we now know that he can drive a car and on the freeway!"

I went to bed!

Sharing His Stage

Tribute to the Late Gregory Hines

One week prior to my son's high school graduation, I was en-route to Palm Springs, to attend a meeting with the board of directors of a time share I had purchased several years earlier. I was on the freeway and passed the Cerritos Performing Arts Center in the City of Cerritos, and noticed their marquee that announced, "Gregory Hines, Coming in June."

I immediately thought, Wow, what a wonderful graduation present this would be for Channing, my eldest son who had been enrolled in the R. D. Colburn's School of Performing Arts since the age of five, studying dance and drums. He had studied under the late Alfred Desio for twelve years and the late Fayard Nicholas of the famed Nicholas brothers for a year.

Channing knew that Alfred and Gregory were friends who worked together on the movie "Tap" in earlier years but he had never asked his teacher if he could be introduced to him.

En-route home, following the meeting in Palm Springs, I stopped and purchased four tickets for the Gregory Hines show. Two days prior to the show I surprised Channing with the tickets and shared my plan with him. Yes, I had a plan and the plan was to arrive one hour early to submit Channing's bio to an usher requesting that he take it directly to Mr. Hines, or to his manager for him to give to Mr. Hines as soon as possible.

The thought of Channing actually dancing for him would have been a miracle. To know that he received his bio would have been exciting enough.

The evening of the show, I asked Channing to take his tap shoes hoping for that miracle. He agreed hesitantly and off we went, along with my friend Laura and her daughter Heather.

We arrived one and a half hours early. It was the perfect night: beautiful facility, lovely weather, great parking (because we were so early), and a nice restaurant across from the Center. As we parked and got out of the car, Channing asked, "Mom should I take my tap shoes?" I said "No, we should probably wait first to see if there is any possible way for you to dance for him tonight."

Channing presented his bio to the usher and made his request known. We had a great meal but our minds and conversation were on the anticipated show. I was actually wondering if I had been presumptuous in thinking we could possibly meet Gregory Hines tonight.

The lights dimmed, the show began with Mr. Hines in his greatest form, dancing the night away with such zeal and zest that no one would think of taking their eyes off of him. Such style, grace and personality flowed from one dance to the next, with songs interspersed from time to time.

I glanced at Channing to capture as many expressions that I could, to be able to hold them in my memory bank for years to come. He was calm externally but I could see that his mind was racing. I could feel him...Wow, if only.

The show was so entertaining that it seemed as though the first half was only 15 or 20 minutes, when in reality it was 50. There was a brief intermission, and then the bell rang to announce the end of it. The lights dimmed, and the show took off again with Mr. Hines performing his rendition of an African tap dance. Concluding that segment, he stopped and began to talk to the audience. He asked if anyone brought along tap shoes, and if so, please come up on stage.

I thought, OH MY GOD WHAT? People of all ages began to shuffle around in their seats putting on their tap shoes. Children ran from the rear of the first floor, excited to dance on stage with one of the greatest tap dancers alive. It appeared as though everyone but Channing and I knew that he would make this appeal.

We found out later that Gregory had placed a call to Lynn Dally, the director of Jazz Tap Ensemble asking her to be prepared to dance during this segment of his show. So there were approximately 15 children between the ages of 5 and 15 and Lynn Dally on the stage with Gregory. He continued to ask "Is there anyone else? Is there anyone else?" He said it so many times that he began to imitate a televangelist. "If you are here today, please come on down."

At this point, Channing looked at me, and I passed him the keys without saying a word. He jumped over the banister. We were seated in the last row of the second level. I'm thankful that we were seated there; otherwise I'm not sure where he would have landed.

He ran down the stairs into the lobby area. The ushers rushed to him to ask if everything was okay. He answered loudly, "Yes, just open the door and leave it open! I'll be right back."

The ushers knew immediately what was going on. They held the door for him and upon his return, ushered him down the east side wall outside of the theatre, opening a side door to the stage area. As Channing entered the stage along with one other person, Mr. Hines asked, "Where have you been? I've been waiting for you."

The audience roared. Laura, Heather and I were nervous wrecks as we sat wondering what would happen next.

Channing ended up standing next to Ms. Dally as Gregory went down the row of dancers asking their names. He stopped to introduce Ms. Dally and next to her stood Channing. When Channing said his name Ms. Dally asked, "You are Channing Holmes, Alfred Desio's student?" "Yes," replied Channing. She went on to tell him that she had heard so many good things about him from Alfred. At that point, Channing was in shock. I sat on the second level watching the two of them chatter on stage. There he stood next to Lynn Dally, one of the most respected dance company directors and Gregory Hines. I'm sure he felt that he couldn't remember dying but surely he was in heaven.

Gregory began to dance a few steps, then stopped and asked the group to repeat his movements. The stage was full of young hopefuls that were in complete disbelief at that moment. Following what I'll call the tap lesson, he allowed each participant to go solo.

This is when the real fun began. What an experience. It was a great moment for each participant and highly entertaining for the audience. Some made us smile, others made us cry from laughter. Okay, at this point Gregory is working his way to stage left, and its Ms. Dally's turn. She danced with grace and charm, never missing a beat. The audience applauded as though they had come to see her perform. It was apparent that the dancers in the audience knew of her celebrity. As for me, I couldn't really relax to enjoy her solo due to praying that Channing would perform well and not over do it, under do it, or break something.

Okay, Channing's up. He slid from one end of the stage to the other, with toe, ball, chain in sequences that had never been seen before. The audience went into thunderous applause. Laura, Heather and I could hear the whispering and talking among the crowd. People around us who saw him jump over the banister, (running to get his shoes), began to ask if that segment of the show was planned. Some actually thought we weren't telling the truth when we answered no.

He was so professional that evening that Gregory began to bow to him, and the audience roared with laughter. Gregory ran to the rear of the stage, got a bottle of water and poured it in the area of the stage where Channing had danced, indicating that it was just too HOT! I could only think about sitting in the halls or in my car for twelve years, week after week, that it all has finally paid off. The audience loved it and appreciated Gregory for extending his show to young aspiring dancers. What an ego boost for all of them.

Channing never returned to his seat that evening until approximately 15 minutes after the show had ended. He finally returned accompanied by Lynn Dally and her assistant Gayle Hooks. They wanted to meet me to give me their cards. Ms. Dally asked if Channing would contact her if he ever wanted to dance professionally. It was extremely flattering, but Channing was scheduled to start his freshman year at Langston University in Oklahoma in two days.

After our brief meeting, we were invited to attend a reception for Gregory. As we arrived at the reception, the one person I was hoping would be in the audience was at the reception, Channing's teacher, Alfred Desio. We had no idea that he was in attendance that evening. He was so pleased with Channing's performance. He said that he was in top form throughout that segment of the show, and he felt that everything he had taught Channing over the years had all come together that evening. We were both very proud of him.

Channing was so high in the clouds at the reception. I asked him to let me carry his tap shoes because I felt he would surely leave them in Cerritos. To my surprise, when Gregory entered the room, he immediately walked over to me. As he approached, I offered my hand to said hello. As he shook my hand I said, "I'm his mother." He said with much charm, "My mother carried my shoes as well," and went on to tell me that she could only afford one dance lesson per week, so when his brother would go to class upon his return home he would teach him new steps. Our meeting was brief but very memorable. Gregory informed me that he had received Channing's bio prior to the show from an usher and that he knew Channing must have been a good dancer if studying under Alfred for 12 years. Then he added that he held up the show as long as he could hoping that Channing would come up to the stage. He couldn't figure out what took him so long, until I told him that his shoes were in the car. We had a big laugh on that one.

After his freshman year at Langston University, Channing returned from college wanting desperately to dance. He was immediately hired by Lynn Dally to join the Jazz Tap Ensemble. He traveled with that troop for several years, leaving only to join "Riverdance the Show," on Broadway, The European Tour and the U.S. Tour.

During one of his breaks from the "Riverdance" production, while teaching at a local dance academy, the owner received a casting call for the Gregory Hines show. She invited Channing to accompany her and her son to the call. Channing was hired to teach several of the cast members tap steps for an upcoming episode of the show.

Later that week, Gregory phoned our home. I answered and held a very long conversation with him, asking if he remembered the Cerritos Show. He said yes, but hadn't figured out that Channing was the same guy. Gregory was delighted to work with Channing on his show and afterwards became a mentor to him referring and recommending him for several job opportunities such as: the Gregory Hines HBO special, "Mr Bojangles"; live fundraising performances, and Martin Scorcese's, "Gangs of New York."

Channing was working on Broadway in "Riverdance on Broadway" at the time of the call for "Gangs." Riverdance released him to go to Europe for three weeks to film the movie, something he had dreamed about. He laughs today as he tells the story of how he stuck closely to Mr. Scorcese during the shoot. People thought he was his security, but Channing was trying to learn all he could about filmmaking within that three week period.

I can specifically remember Gregory calling our home. He left a message on our answer machine once of him singing Happy Birthday to Channing. He sang the entire song and ended it by singing the last line to me, "and it's all because of Ruth." Oh Lord, I wanted to call all my friends and let them listen to the message....and I did call some.

Approximately two years later, I got up one morning with the intention of going to visit one of my closest friends, Karla who lived in Santa Monica. As I was dressing, the spirit of God spoke to me through a thought and said, you will meet Gregory Hines for the second time today. It seemed to be just a passing thought, but I asked myself why and how would I meet him?

I didn't think anything more about it. As I arrived in Santa Monica that morning, my friend and I went on Main Street for breakfast. As we walked from the restaurant we passed a small convenience store. I looked inside and there stood Gregory Hines in the very rear of the store reading a newspaper. It appeared as though he had just stopped in for a moment during his morning jog to check out an article.

I walked into the store and stopped about seven feet from him to make sure it was really him. I said "Hello Mr. Hines, is that you?" He slowly, very slowly looked up from the magazine, or a newspaper, and said yes. I said "Hello, I'm Channing's mother." He immediately returned the publication to the stand, walked over to me and gave me the greatest bear hug I had ever received. We talked at length. Afterwards I told him that I had been informed that I would meet him on this day. He seemed a bit startled but never stopped being the charming gentleman that he was.

Later one Sunday we were in church when I was called out of the service for a phone call. It was my friend Karla, calling to tell me of Mr. Hines' transition. She said she called because she didn't want Channing to hear of his passing over the radio while driving home that day. She knew that they had grown to be great friends. It was one of the hardest things I've ever had to tell him. God sends angels into our lives, doesn't He?!

A Kodak Moment

Part Two of "Church Meeting"

In September 1997, I went to lunch alone to the deli section of the Von's Supermarket in Inglewood to order Chinese food. After lunch I decided to pick up a few groceries, casually browsing through the vegetable section. While picking up sweet potatoes and onions, a very soft voice said, "Turn around." As I turned I could see a male image standing a few feet behind me. As I focused I could see it was my estranged husband Kenneth, whom I had not seen in seven years and four months.

He was well groomed and just standing there with his hand on his hip staring in awe at me. Realizing who he was, I carefully placed the bags of sweet potatoes and onions in the child's seat of the shopping cart and walked toward what appeared to be a mirage. I wasn't sure what was about to happen but when I got within reach, I embraced him as he continued to stand there like a statue. Finally he asked, "You don't have a knife do you?" I said, "No." That broke the ice. He began to hug me back and we talked and talked and talked. My heart was beating so rapidly, and I could tell his was also. I asked him if he would please come over to meet his son for the first time. He agreed and did so that very evening at 8:30 p.m. following work.

Needless to say it was very difficult for me to get anything done that afternoon. I felt as though I had fallen asleep at home during my lunch hour and dreamt the entire scenario. But it was real, so real that I can actually see the entire scene today, twelve years later.

Before I forget, Kenneth didn't purchase a thing from the store that day. After our supermarket meeting, it took all of his strength to walk straight out the door back to his car. As for me, I mustered up enough strength to purchase my sweet potatoes and onions but not much more than that.

As he entered our home that evening, we began to ponder how we would introduce him to his son. He said, "Don't ask me. I just stopped for two beers to get up enough nerve to come over here. What have you been telling the boy anyway?"

"Only good things. All positive things," I replied. I asked if he would remain in the front of the house while I went to the family room to prepare Lladon for the introduction. Before the door bell rang, I saw him from the window approaching the front door so I rushed to the family room to tell Channing, my oldest son, that he had arrived. Channing was excited to see Kenneth again. He tried later to explain to me how fast his heart began to beat once I said that his step dad was actually back and here in the house, after being away for several years.

I told Lladon that someone was here to see him. Someone whom he would really like to see. He began to name friends like Michelle, and some of his other little friends. I finally said, "It's your daddy. "My daddy" he exclaimed, his eyes enlarged. I answered, "Yes," as I grabbed his hand. I asked him to come with me to meet him. Kenneth was seated, and as we turned the corner of the atrium, with Channing following closely behind, his first comments were, "He looks like you Ruth." They hugged and sort of pushed each other back hoping to get a better look. Then Kenneth looked at his stepson, now standing taller than Kenneth at age 19 and asked, "Bullet! (the name he had given him fourteen years earlier) Is that you?"

It was an awesome three hours of talking and getting reacquainted. He began to explain what had happened in his life for the past seven years and how he had to live. I won't go there. Not!! He asked for forgiveness from all of us. We were all very quiet, just listening as he spoke. Throughout the evening, I would say comical things in hopes of preventing tears. I wanted no tears that evening, maybe later.

We all walked Kenneth to his car to say good night. Lladon rode on the shoulders of his big brother while big brother carried a box I had maintained over the years for Kenneth. These were personal things he had left behind, photos from his childhood, a nice watch and other items I can't recall. The boys left us to talk. We said things that were needed and he agreed to return soon.

He phoned the next day saying that he simply wanted to check my work number before he placed it permanently in his phone book...sounded like an excuse to call to me.

After my husband's departure, Channing asked his little brother what were his thoughts after seeing his dad for the very first time, his response was, "It was a Kodak moment Chan."

From that point on in 1997 until today, they are the best of friends. God does answer the effectual prayers of children and Sunday school teachers.

Burnie and Ardie Cook with sons Lloyd and baby Donald (1943)

Big Brothers Lloyd and Donald
with baby sister Ruth (1950)

My first professional singing group (1966).
Ruth, Brenda Peppars Underwood, Brenda Piggee

Sons Channing and Lladon (1993)

How Do I End This Sermon?

My five year old son, Lladon, had been very active in his Sunday school class since the age of three, the acceptable age for Children's Church and Sunday school at our church. He would come home trying to recite stories that his teacher, Mrs. Mullin had shared that Sunday morning.

By the age of five, I noticed that he was really retaining the information that she was teaching so I decided to teach him the story of Ruth, thinking that it would be of interest to him since my name was Ruth.

I read it to him twice, stopping to carefully pronounce the names of each character. Once he felt comfortable with the story he went to Mrs. Mullin and told her that he knew the story of Ruth. That very Sunday she requested that he tell the story to his class. He proudly walked to the front of the class and recited the story without a hitch. I was in the main sanctuary, unable to hear how he actually ended the story.

A few weeks passed and Youth Day at our church was approaching. This is the day that the youth of the congregation are in charge of the worship service and one young person would be selected to present a message prior to our pastor's message. Lladon had done such a good job presenting the story of Ruth to his classmates that Mrs. Mullin requested that he should present the story to the congregation.

He gladly accepted the invitation. As for me, I was a wreak, thinking that he would forget several of the names, since they were not the usual little friends names that he was familiar with. I had to come up with things to help him remember each name such as: she owed me for Naomi, Eli and me for Elimelech, one of the Wayon brothers for Mahlon, chili for Chilion, Oprah on TV for Orpah, Boaz for Boaz and their son went to bed for Obed. Ruth, I wasn't worried about. I knew he had that one totally memorized, but the others, I was afraid for him.

The Sunday prior to Youth Day, we reviewed the story. Lladon was prepared and ready to go.

It's now Sunday morning and he is introduced to the congregation by Mrs. Mullin, as our special speaker today. He walks to the front of the church and the pastor asked if he would like the mike to be on a stand of if he would like to be able to walk and hold the microphone. He chose to walk with a hand mike, as the congregants began to chuckle.

I had dressed him in his nicest suit. It was black, his shirt was white with a multicolored tie, and he looked just like a minister.

He began the story, walking across the front of the church and emulating his uncle Donald, the pastor, with pride in his stride. People were amazed as he presented the story without any breaks or hesitations. He spoke loudly and clearly as he continued to pace back and forth, leaving the attendees desiring more and more from him.

As he geared up for his conclusion, it occurred to me that we had not determined how he would end the story prior to returning to his seat. I panicked and thought "Now what? He's done such a great job with the story. He's going to blow it all by not knowing how to end it."

But he never looked over at me for help or with an "Oh my God, What am I to do?" look. He calmly said, Ruth married Boaz and they had a baby and named him Obed and her mother-in-law, Naomi helped her to care for him. And they lived happily ever after!

The End!

Remove the Floatation Devices

In the summer of 1996, I coordinated a family retreat to Rancho Mirage, California for our congregation. We had planned special outings for the membership of the church usually every two years. That particular year we stayed at The Oasis Hotel.

Prior to this trip, my six year old had accompanied me to our timeshare in Palm Springs each year since his birth. We would always take one or two of his cousins, Donald and Barrington, and sometimes his older brother Channing. All of them could swim very well, but he would be the only one with all the floatation gear, forearms bubbled, donut around the waist and anything else I could find that would keep him afloat. It wasn't that he was fearful the fact is that I was. Being unable to swim myself caused me to be fearful for him.

One afternoon some of the ladies met with their children to allow them fun time at the pool. They had a great time, but me and one other mother, Darnell were nervous wrecks. Neither of us could swim, so both of our sons were the only two with all the gear.

The very next afternoon, I had volunteered to drive some of the senior ladies around for a brief sightseeing trip, out and about Palm Springs. Darnell wanted to go along with me, however our sons Lladon and Skylar wanted to stay with the other children and play in the pool. Darnell and I were very uncomfortable with the idea of leaving them, even though Pat and Cathy, two of our friends and church members agreed to remain with them at all times.

We finally drug ourselves away from the boys, but leaving with fear in our hearts. We were gone for approximately one and a half hours, but I couldn't really enjoy the tour for worrying about our little fellows.

Upon our return as we approached the pool area, we noticed that the boys were smiling and talking with Pat and Cathy. I entered the area with relief written all over my face, not from Rolaids, even though I probably needed a few as I left, but just from seeing that they were okay.

As Darnell and I walked closer to Pat and Cathy, they began to say, "The boys want you to have a seat, they would like to show you something." We sat down hesitantly on the lounge chairs at the opposite end of the pool. As soon as we sat down they dived into the water and swam to us without pausing, stopping or speaking. Darnell and I were amazed and neither of us could speak.

When Lladon got out of the water he said, "Mom, I told you I could swim." I repeat I couldn't speak. Darnell was in worse shape than I. She looked panic-stricken. All we could do was hug them and brag on how proud we were of their accomplishment.

We were told that Pat and Cathy worked with them—first removing all floatation devices, teaching them to keep their heads above the water, breathing techniques and the strokes. Within one and a half hours, it all came together.

The boys were so excited to show us that they could swim. We sat another 20 or 30 minutes watching them go back and forth in the pool. My eyes stayed focused on Lladon's smile. He was thrilled.

He had asked me two summers before if he could remove the floaties and I would always say, "Not until you learn how to swim." Now how much sense did that make? He couldn't learn because he had on too much stuff!

We left Rancho Mirage the following afternoon, which was a Saturday. Upon our arrival to church the next day Lladon and Skylar couldn't wait to tell their Sunday school teacher, Mrs. Mullin, what had occurred during their trip. They rushed to her to tell the good news, no not the gospel, but that they had learned how to swim. She was one that would really be excited for the children about anything that they accomplished, so she went on and on with hugs and praises. As I watched them explain every bit of their experience to her, I couldn't help but wonder what else I had possibly prevented him from learning or doing due to my fears.

Left Hand Catch

My youngest son, Lladon had just turned six and began to express a desire to enter Little League Baseball. As a single mom, I knew that meant long hours at the local baseball field with other parents and children. It was something I really didn't look forward to. I was an indoors person myself, but I knew it would be good for his motor skills.

My oldest son and I went out to purchase additional items we felt he would need to give him more confidence, items such as a batting glove and a right hand fielder's glove. He was so excited to be a part of the team.

Week after week, we would spend Saturday mornings on Getty Field in Inglewood. His coaches were fathers of two of the players on the team. Because I was a novice at baseball's Little League, I was surprised to learn how serious this game was to parents and coaches. I thought it would just be for fun. No way! The attendees were as serious as they would have been attending an L.A. Dodger's baseball game and would have placed a wager on the game.

Each week the coaches became more and more stern. Because of their harshness, I became uncomfortable with taking him. Not only did they make me uncomfortable, but they also annoyed the referees.

At one of the games, early in the season, the referee kicked the coaches off the field and one of the player's father had to take over our team for the remainder of the game. It was coincidental that this particular father was one of our neighbors and our sons often played together. He was one with a caring spirit and kind personality.

My son held his own at the games but nothing seemed good enough for these coaches. The games had become a chore for me. I became weary from trying to explain to him how important it was not to act like his coaches. I felt like his spirit had been broken.

One day the pitcher threw a ball and accidentally hit my son. That's when the fun began. From that point, every time he got up to bat he would dodge the ball, not only when up to bat but out in the field too. If a fly ball would come near him he would dodge it. There he was jumping from left to right. After the ball would hit the ground, he would run, pick it up and throw it to anyone he thought should have it. People began to snicker each time he would go up to bat, awaiting his two step, dodge step.

We were nearing the end of the season and this win would allow them to enter the playoffs. Here we go again. In the middle of the game both coaches were kicked out of the game and off the field, leaving an unprepared father to take over.

The children were devastated, wondering who to listen to, their two coaches who were standing behind the bleachers screaming like idiots, or their teammates' father, who was nearby. Yes, it was a mess! There I was in total distress hoping that my son would not be the one to blow this game by playing dodge ball.

I began to pray. My son's team was leading 4 to 3 in the bottom of the last inning with the other team at bat. As the last batter got up my thoughts were, if Lladon blows this game we may need a police escort out of the park. At this point, I was convinced that this was not going to be the sport for my little boy...just too much pressure.

As the ball was hit by the opponent, it was a fly ball that went exactly my son's arm length, to the left of his shoulder. No one else was near him or the ball. The inexperienced coach stood up from the bench. We could all see that it was his ball and only his. The coach yelled very slowly, but in a loud but kind voice, "Lladon catch the ball."

As I sat saying to myself, just stick your left arm out as far as you can and grip the ball when it falls into your glove. It was like a magic trick in slow motion. He stuck his left arm out, the ball fell directly into his glove and he held on to it with pride. All we could see were expressions of anguish and delight on his little face. Everyone in the bleachers stood up and screamed, jumped and applauded.

On the way home from the game he was still shaken. He said to me that he desired to replace baseball with another sport. Those were words that I had longed to hear from him. The team made the playoffs, but lost the championship. The confidence in his potential athletic ability acquired from that game sustained him throughout junior and senior high in basketball. Kudos to the three coaches, the two crazy ones and the one with sense!

CHAPTER FOUR

MY FAITH

New Home Before Glory

My parents purchased their home in 1953 and lived there until I moved them in with me and my family in 1988. I remember praying for three years asking God for a home large enough for my parents and family to live together. My parents had begun to develop illnesses that required around the clock attention. My father had cancer and my mother had developed Parkinson's and beginning stages of Alzheimer Disease.

They had literally stopped eating. I would cook and prepare meals and take containers of food to their home on Monday that were to last until Wednesday. I would prepare them like they were TV dinners. Upon my return on Wednesday, the food would not have been touched. When I consulted with physicians I was told that it was time to either have someone live with them or move them in with me. I choose the second option. I had been praying for three years asking God for a home large enough for all of us, my parents, my husband and I, and our pre-teen son.

While driving to the store one day, about two blocks from my home I saw a lovely house that was for sale. I phoned the broker and later met with him to walk through the house. It was nice but not quit large enough. However I wanted to move my parents so badly I made a bid on the house.

The next week I was scheduled to take my down payment to the broker at the house that was soon to be mine, I thought. Upon my arrival, the broker's car was parked in front of the house but no one would answer the door. I went back home in tears, phoned the broker, left several messages, never hearing from him. My husband could see my despair. After several hours he simply said, "Ruth, this is not your house."

He was correct. Within two weeks I left home en-route to visit my friend Georgia, who lived not very far from me. I slowly drove down streets hoping to see "For Sale" signs out on lawns. This particular day was my day to be blessed! As I drove down Fifth Avenue in Inglewood, there was a sign that read, "Help You Sell" in front of a lovely home that appeared to be very large. I stopped long enough to write down the phone number and as I was writing I could see a lady looking out of the kitchen window.

I'm now in a hurry to get to my friend Georgia's house to call the number. I phoned the office only to be told that they had no record of that listing. In addition, no one in the office had listed a home in Inglewood. My son Channing was with me. He and I immediately left Georgia's home and drove back to the house on Fifth Avenue. I wanted to be sure that I had correctly recorded the phone number to the office. It was correct. As I parked in front to double check, I asked my son if he would go to the door and ask the owner if I could speak with her about the house because the listing agent did not have any information about it. He was twelve at the time and I am not sure what he said to the lady who answered the door but he soon signaled for me to get out of the car. I literally wanted to run to the door.

The lady greeted me and invited me into her home. I began to explain to her that no one in the office had information on the listing. She explained that prior to me driving by the first time, she had just signed the contract and that the broker was not to submit the listing info to the office clerk for processing until the next morning.

She went on to say that as I drove by, she was on the phone speaking with her sister in Texas and said, "I believe the new owner of my house just drove by." After I told her that I wanted a place large enough to bring my parents to live with my family, she allowed me to have a walk-through. It was beautifully decorated with four bedrooms, two full bathrooms, a large dining room with a very large family room that led to a huge backyard that had several trees and a tool shed large enough to walk around in.

She had added several rooms and it appeared to be her dream home. She explained that she loved the house but that her son who had problems committed suicide in the house several months earlier. Then I understood why she would want to walk away from such a beautiful home.

I returned the next day with my husband and parents. Everyone loved the house and the process began. We were on a time frame. In order for her to acquire the home she wanted in Texas, she needed the funding that her Inglewood house would provide. In the meantime my mortgage broker's son became ill and threw off the entire schedule by one week. We were both very nervous wondering if we would be able to make it all work, me acquiring her home and her being able to arrive in Texas in enough time to close her deal.

The home she purchased was a Texas mansion and no other Blacks lived in the area. People were standing in line hoping that she wouldn't be able to purchase it. God worked for me again. Clerks in the mortgage office worked for hours on my loan. The day she arrived in Texas was her deadline date. She left the Inglewood house finally after moving items from her garage into three moving vans. As she was moving her items out of the house through the back door, I was moving items into the house through the front door. It was like magic. Strangers were stopping to ask if we wanted to sell anything. Furniture was all over the front lawn.

I can remember Mrs. Mercy McDonald and Mrs. Jerline Blanton, two of the ladies from our church, coming over to assist me with the move. Wow, could they work. People that were on hand to help the original owner with her move thought that Mrs. McDonald and Mrs. Blanton where there to assist her but soon found out that they were there to help me move in. They loved my mother and had worked with her for years building Harvest Church and I just happened to be a recipient of their love for our family.

My family loved their new home. We moved in August of 1988. I gave my mother a party that December to celebrate her 72nd birthday. Many of her friends were on hand to celebrate this special day. I'll never forget how excited she was to show her friends around her new home.

A short time following our move, I recall going to Home Depot, a new store for the area, and walking through it purchasing a large number of light bulbs, at least 15, and many other household items needed for our new home. My money was very limited, because I had put all I had into the down payment on the house. As I got about halfway finished shopping, it dawned on me that I had no money, no cash and my credit card was maxed. A soft voice said, "Continue to shop." I obeyed but began to walk around the store much slower, trying to figure out how I was going to purchase all the items that had filled my basket. I was thinking, "Okay, no cash, no credit card, why am I here?"

As I walked passed the first cashier, I was trying to decide if I would just leave the basket in the front of the store near an exit, return all the items to their specific aisles or walk to the rear of the store to leave the filled basket. As I got closer to the second cashier a young lady walked up to me and said, "Hello, may I interest you in applying for a credit card with Home Depot? We are new in the area and would like to have you as a regular customer." My immediate thought was, lady if you only knew. I can't pay for what I have. She continued with her well prepared presentation. It wasn't until she said, "If you sign up for a credit card today, you won't have to pay for today's purchase until your first statement arrives in the mail." I completed the application as quickly as I could, smiling and thanking God the entire time for another miracle. He had come through for me again. After that favor, my faith was moving to higher heights.

My father passed away after the first year. He really enjoyed bonding with his grandson in their tool shed in the backyard. My mother enjoyed her new residence for nine years prior to leaving for glory.

Tears For Spain

After studying with the same dance teacher for nine years from age 5 to 14, my son Channing was pulled from his dance troop to become the teacher's dance partner, something he had dreamed about for years.

In 1996, he was asked to accompany his teacher, the late Alfred Desio and his wife Louise Reichlin to Barcelona, Spain to participate in the city's annual dance festival. We had been assured that the hotel would be expensed through an arts grant but I would be responsible for his flight. I saved and scraped for weeks for the cost of the flight, which was $1,000. As a single mom, I didn't have very much, but the thought of him being invited to participate in such an event assured me that it would be worth it to rob Peter AND Paul.

As the date drew closer, we were once again reassured that the hotel expense would be provided for from the grant. Channing was so excited to be able to travel abroad, especially without a parent but with his teacher, mentor and friend Alfred.

My brother who is also our pastor shared the information about the trip with our congregation two weeks prior to the departure date. Everyone was so happy for Channing. I prayed and pondered all day Saturday without a single thought as to how I would secure the balance for the trip if the grant would be denied.

Sunday morning we arrived at church at our usual time, prepared to serve as usual, with Channing on drums and me in the choir. As my brother began to deliver his sermon, a choir member seated three people away from me, passed a note to me that read, "Does Channing need anything for his trip?" signed, Barbara.

I immediately replied by note that stated, "Barbara, it's confirmed, Chan leaves for Spain one week from tomorrow, 9 a.m., that is if an arts grant is approved for the hotel fees. I paid for the flight $1,000 plus, but was hoping that an arts grant that we had applied for will cover the hotel signed, Ruth. Then I added a P.S. that read, 9 days in Spain at $35 per night, not sure what I'm going to do.

A few moments later, a tithe envelope was passed to me again from Barbara. By now everyone on our pew in the choir was wondering what was going on? Enclosed in the envelope was a check in the amount of $315 and a note that stated, "In the event the grant doesn't come through." It was the exact amount needed to complete all financial needs for the trip.

I began to cry as I read the amount line on the check. For some reason my brother happened to turn to the choir, just in time to see tears rolling from my eyes.

Following worship service that morning he asked me, "How was my sermon?" I wondered why he was asking. All I could say was "It was good." Knowing that I hadn't heard one word of the sermon that day, I asked, "Why are you asking?" "Because I saw you crying and thought, Wow, this must be a touching message today, because you never cry during my sermons," he replied.

I could not bring myself to tell him I wasn't crying because his sermon had touched me, I was crying for Spain! The very next day we received word that the grant for the hotel expense ($350.00) had been denied! Oftentimes God is not on time but early.

Shoes

I had recently accepted a position that didn't require that I wear heels to work. This was good news; however all I had were high heels after being a part of corporate America for so many years. At the time I had a roommate, Laura, who was going to visit her parents in Colorado. Prior to her departure, I remember walking down the hallway to my bedroom asking God for shoes, flat shoes, to wear to my new job.

Laura visited with her parents for about ten days. Early in the evening of the first night upon her return home, she called me into her room to show me what her mother had given to her. When I walked into her room there were five pairs of the cutest flat shoes. If I had had the money or opportunity I would have picked out all five. She said, "Look at the shoes my mother gave me." My mouth flew open as I yelled your mother? I couldn't believe her mother's taste was so close to Laura's and mine. She had often told me how beautifully her mother dressed and seeing those shoes convinced me.

I remember admiring each pair, picking them up, feeling the leather, commenting on the styles, even trying on a couple. Laura smiled as we agree that her mother had great taste.

As I exited the room, heading toward my bedroom, I distinctly remember looking up and saying, "Lord I asked you for shoes, flat shoes. Laura didn't ask you for shoes, heels or flats. It was me, Ruth!" A few days went by as I continued to wonder how I was going to get the shoes I needed.

One day not too long after Laura had returned from her visit, she called me into her room and said, "The shoes my mother gave me hurt my feet. Would you like to have them?" My immediate response was "Yes, thank you. With a huge smile on my face, I added, "They are perfect for my new job." She handed me all five pair. I strolled down the hallway en-route to my closet, looking up, grinning at this point, saying, "Thank you Lord for answering another prayer." I wore all five pair for several years.

After about three years, I returned to corporate America by landing a job with a third national thrift, requiring heels again. By this time, I was in need of heels. After approximately one month on the job, a friend called. Dorothy said that a lady on her job was cleaning out her closet and had four pairs of heels that were like new. She told her co-worker that she couldn't think of anyone that wore a size seven and a half shoe size.

But after several days I popped into her mind, well we know who did that, and she called to confirm my shoe size and it was my size. Dorothy brought me a pair of green suede, 2-inch heels along with a pair of tan, black, and beige leather heels to church from her co-worker.

Shortly thereafter, I took six pairs of heels to church that I could no longer wear—too tight, too wide, bad fit, nothing in the closet to match the color, etc. Ladies were rushing to the fellowship hall to see if any would work for them. Those that lucked out were as thankful as I was when I received blessings from Laura and Dorothy.

We have not, because we ask not. Ladies, ask and it shall be given unto you, "SHOES!"

The Bus Vouchers

(As appeared in "Chicken Soup for the African American Woman's Soul," Publication)

Leaving home for work late one day near the end of December, I missed my normal bus and had to catch the later one. I checked my watch and knew I could still make it on time, but I was cutting it close—a stressful start to the morning.

As I sat waiting for the bus, I realized that the end of the month meant the beginning of a new one, which meant it was time to buy my bus pass for January, a cost of $100. Mind you, that was $100 that I didn't have. The holidays had just passed, my husband was unemployed at the time and things were very tight for our family. I signed audibly. If I couldn't get to work, things would only get worse.

Seeing no other viable options, I began to pray and ask God to help me solve this problem, to send me the money to meet this need, as I had done in the past for other things. I offered my problem to God, which if nothing else, made me feel better and more prepared to face my day.

Continuing to pray, I rode past one bus stop. At the second stop, a lady got on the bus whom I had met several weeks prior. She and I often took the same bus home in the evening and had shared scriptures and conversations together about ways to share God with co-workers. Happy to see her, I smiled.

As she reached my seat, she said, "Good morning, I have something for you." I thought perhaps she had a passage she wanted to read to me or a book she wanted to share. She sat down and, whispering across the person between us, asked if the company I worked for paid for my transportation. An odd question, I thought, especially in light of my recent concerns, but I let her know that they did not.

She had the person sitting between us pass me an envelope. I opened the envelope and there were bus vouchers for the months of January, February and part of March—worth $226! I can only imagine how surprised I must have looked. God had certainly answered my prayers before, and I trusted that he would again, but I didn't expect it to happen so quickly and efficiently, immediately after uttering the prayer!

I looked up at her speechless and she explained, "I accepted a position in Texas and will be moving there within a few days. I pre-purchased these bus vouchers and they are nonrefundable. I didn't want them to go to waste, so when I prayed over what the best thing to do with them was, spirit told me to give the bus vouchers to you. I took an earlier bus than I normally do, hoping to see you this morning."

Obviously, God had been working on the solution even before I recognized the problem. We cried together, all the way to work, when we recognized how clearly we were both a part of God's plan.

This turned out to be the perfect way for me to share God with my co-workers as, needless to say, I shared the testimony with whomever I could find that would listen.

Prayer for Niche

My husband Mark and I met in June of 2001, dated 14 months and decided to marry, August 2002. He and I both had teenage sons from previous marriages. My son lived with me and Mark's son lived with his mother. My son did not meet his father until he was seven.

During our courtship we discussed having Mark's son come to live with us after we marry. There wouldn't be a problem raising two boys together. We could see that they really got along exceptionally well. The problem would come from fighting our way through the fact that neither had previously had a male authority figure in their homes and that they had hoped in their hearts that each set of parents would find a way to reunite. I had been so caught up in the courtship that I totally missed all the signs of discontent and anguish that they were enduring.

There was a section of the wedding ceremony that we had asked each of them to participate in honoring their grandparents by saying, "We honor our grandparents today, James, Mary, Ardie and Burnie. They are not with us physically but we know that they are in spirit." As they both participated in presenting this statement I turned to look at them. It was only then that I was able to see the pain that they shared. Neither of the boys ever verbalized that they hoped we would return to our spouses but their actions and countenance spoke louder than words.

At that very moment as I looked at the two of them together, ages 12 and 13 ½, I knew immediately that I would have a lot of work before me in blending our families.

The first school year was rough. School grades were down and ugly dispositions were daily challenges. My son was the one with the open anxiety who would periodically want to fight. Mark's son would misbehave in school, causing meetings called with teachers and school counselors. I sought counsel from anyone that I thought knew anything about blending families.

One day when I had gotten to my wits end, I remember stopping, praying and asking God for help in making our family a unit of love and peace. I began to feel that if the boys could find something that they would enjoy, it would take their minds off of being miserable during this time of adjustment.

Mark is a kind and very considerate person, willing to do anything to make things work for all of us and I tried as hard to be a person who would be thought of as a mom and not a stepmom.

My prayer was, "Lord if you would help our sons find their niche for this period of their lives, Mark and I would be so appreciative." I finally got to the point where I thought that my marriage would fall apart if things didn't change.

After a few weeks of continued prayer, my son joined the basketball team at his junior high school and Mark's son joined the wrestling team at his high school. Things began to change, not overnight, but gradually.

All of the anxiety and frustration was taken out on the basketball court and the gym floor wrestling mat. I began to feel sorry for their opponents. My husband and I would attend the basketball games and wrestling matches. The wrestling matches became so intense I refused to continue to go. I would leave stressed from worrying if my stepson or his opponent would end up hurt.

As for the basketball player, upon entering high school the following year, he was invited to join the varsity team as a 9th grader. Wow, did that boost his ego.

Today, I can say that I'm thankful for basketball, wrestling matches and the fact that prayer works!

Is It My Turn Yet?

At the age of three, my nephew Mark's motor skills and speaking ability were below the level of a three year old. He was diagnosed as a special child, no specific category other than special and indeed he was our special gift. Our love for him and his mother grew daily.

Mark had the ability to dissect small toys trying to understand the mechanism of how they were able to move, make sounds and or flash lights. Then he would meticulously put them back together again, never once damaging or destroying any of their parts.

His mother's maternal grandfather was the pastor of a Baptist church and her father was the pastor of a Charismatic church, both filled weekly with gospel music at it's finest. His mother, grandmother and aunts were lead singers in the church choirs.

By the age of four, Mark began to demonstrate a rejection for gospel music that was performed in the church, not gospel CD's that were played in his home, radio stations or TV channels showcasing the latest releases in gospel music. It was only in church during worship service. I must also interject that Mark had his own transistor radio and tape player in his room, which he would listen to rock, pop and any other kind of music that he wanted to sing along with or dance to. It was just something about the church choir.

He would scream and try to fight with anyone who tried to remove him from the church sanctuary as the choir would sing. He acted as though the music was hurting his ears. He would hold his head or cover his ears and scream as loudly as he could. I can't begin to describe how this would disrupt the service.

Our family began to fervently pray for Mark and seek guidance on how to handle the situation. His reaction to the choir's singing lasted for quite some time. But my niece never stopped taking him to church, nor did we ever stop praying for him.

One Friday afternoon, I received a call from Mark's mother inviting me to a concert featuring the youth choir of the church she attended. I agreed to attend and arrived at 6:25 p.m., allowing time to park and get a good seat for the 7:00 p.m. concert.

Upon my arrival I asked if she wanted to have Mark sit with me during the concert. She smiled and said "Oh no thanks, things are under control." I wondered what she meant by that.

As the congregation gathered and was seated, the music began for the choir's processional. I looked over at Mark's mother and grandmother and they just looked back at me and smiled. I had no idea what was about to happen.

Approximately twenty-six youth between the ages of 9 and 15 marched into the sanctuary wearing beautiful white robes with red mandarin-styled collars and red strips on the sleeves, proudly maintaining an arms length distance between the person in front of them. They sang with blending melodies as though they were adults. What a proud moment it was for all of them.

As the last choir member entered, I could hear the doors closing. As I looked back, to my surprise Mark had entered the sanctuary enrobed as all the other youth, singing and keeping up with the line, trying hard not to bump into the person in front of him. I was so surprised that I could not speak. My niece just looked at me and said, "Surprise!" Tears of joy began to flow from my eyes so rapidly that all the tissue in my purse could not absorb them.

The concert was wonderful. Each lead singer rendered his or her solo with much pride. It was simply delightful being among the parents of the participants.

During the concert, I could see Mark whispering to the young man seated next to him. I wondered why he continued to lean closer to him and whisper after each song. Then the mistress of ceremony announced that there were two more songs remaining prior to the conclusion of the concert. Again Mark whispered.

The emcee returned to the microphone to introduce the final song. She stated that their final selection would be "Jesus Be a Fence All Around Me Everyday," led by Mark.

As he approached the microphone, the congregation and guests went into a thunderous roar with applauses from the little children to adults. He sang as though he had led songs for several years and he never missed a beat or lyric. I was in shock. This was the big surprise. The processional was enough for me to rejoice about, but the solo, I was speechless.

As we exited the sanctuary a lady walked up to Mark's mom and asked if she was actually his mother and stated that the evening had been very special for her because she also had a special child and seeing Mark perform had given her hope. My niece hugged her and said that through prayer there's hope.

Mark is now 22, a high school graduate attending college, employed and singing duets in the young adult choir.

As for the whispering that was between each song during the concert, well Mark was asking, "Is it my turn yet?"

Prayer Equals Baby

I was introduced to Sonia by a mutual friend on the bus one evening en-route home from work. The three of us worked in a high rise in downtown Los Angeles and commuted from West Covina daily on the freeway flyer called "The Silver Streak."

None of us were aware that Sonia and I lived in the same complex until I needed a lift home from the bus stop one day. As she drove into the facility she mentioned that Sonia lived there as well.

Several weeks later, I ran into Sonia on the bus again. This time she was with her husband who also rode the bus to work in downtown Los Angeles. She introduced us and from time to time her husband, Stephen and I, would end up on the same bus going to work.

One day while riding home with Sonia and making small talk, I began asking her questions about why she and Stephen had no children. I thought of them as being the perfect couple, young, attractive, home, cars, dogs, but no babies.

She responded by saying that they wanted children but she had not been able to carry them. After entering the parking lot of our complex, prior to parting, I asked if I could pray for her, not really sure how she would feel about that question. She quickly asked, "And what is your religion?" I replied immediately, "Christian." Then she said okay. I prayed a quick prayer and exited the car.

It was Wednesday and a bible class was scheduled at my home that very evening. As our guests arrived—approximately seven in attendance—prior to starting the class I made the request for prayer for this couple, that God would bless them with a baby. As we closed our session, the class prayed together in agreement for Sonia and Stephen.

I wasn't sure why I wanted to see them with a child so badly. It was possibly because I knew how much joy children can bring to a couple. I continued to pray for them several times during my personal prayer time.

A couple of months later, I ran into Sonia and Stephen at our community mail box area. I was walking and they were leaving with his parents on the way to the car. It was Saturday before Father's Day and I recall saying, "Enjoy the weekend and Happy Father's Day one day Stephen." They all smiled. It really slipped out and I wondered later if I had offended them.

Several months passed and one day Sonia shared with me that she was a diabetic and the extent of her illness. I had no idea that she was ill. I began to doubt my prayers and reasoned with myself to determine why God had not answered our prayers for them.

Could it have been because she was ill and He didn't want the possibility of the baby developing an illness due to the mother's condition? Or was it possible that it would be too difficult for Stephen to care for both his wife and a newborn baby. My thoughts went wild, not really knowing why because He says that our thoughts are not His thoughts.

Once again I ran into Sonia on the bus in June 2008. As we walked to our cars, located in the park and ride area, she happily announced to me, with a bright smile, "Did I tell you that we are having a baby?" I immediately went into shock and said, "WHAT?"

She explained to me that her husband's sister agreed to carry their child. She was the mother of two young children. I had read stories about such pregnancies but to know someone who would actually go through with it was amazing to me. We only had a short time to discuss the matter, but I was in such shock thinking back on my prayers, wondering how, if and when he would answer, I couldn't think of much to say to her.

Approximately four to five months later, my husband Mark and I were entering into a new Target Store that had recently opened in our neighborhood. We ran into Sonia and in her shopping cart was a small baby carrier. I walked over to her, in shock again, and asked if the infant in the carrier was her baby. She smiled and said yes, that, "This was her first outing, a visit to Target." I asked if I could see the baby, and Sonia began to remove a thin pink blanket from around the baby's neck and head. She was the most beautiful little girl I believe I had ever seen. She had a full head of dark curly hair, the perfect size, totally filled-in with plump legs, beautiful blue eyes and so happy. She just looked up at me and smiled, as if to say, I arrived safely.

I remember leaving the store in complete wonderment of God's power through prayer. When I got home I began to call the attendees of the Bible class who prayed with me for this miracle. Each person was as grateful as I was that another prayer had been answered.

CHAPTER 5

JUST FOR FUN

Sing Vickie, Just Sing

A very close friend of mine was embarking on a career in show business as a singer. She has a good voice, great personality and gifted in fashion coordination. She had appeared at several hot spots in the Los Angeles area, singing the most recent hits, accompanied by background singers and musicians. I had been invited to her shows on several occasions but hadn't been able to attend.

One afternoon she called to invite me to what was called a marathon show that she would be appearing on. I thought I'd better attend, since I had not made any previous performances. She volunteered to pick me up, to make sure I'd show up, I guess. We arrived at the club one hour prior to the start of the show and I remained in the dressing room while she prepared for the evening.

The show kicked off with a female comedian, followed by a male singer, then a male comedian and next, a female singer, without any accompanying background. I was tired after the first half. The announcer informed the audience that there would be a 15 minute break then part two of the marathon would begin shortly after. I deliberately sat in the rear of the room to get a full view of everything. My job was to give her details on everything prior to her performance as well as following it. I'm good at that and went prepared to watch every move.

A few seconds before the start of part two, a group of people walked in and sat at a table, up front and dead center of the room. There was a man, in his twenties, two young ladies and an elderly gentleman who looked to be in his 70s. Vicki remained in the dressing room throughout the show until she was called.

It was time for the show to begin once again. The first act was a female comedian who was really funny. About midway through her performance she began to include the senior gentleman up front into her act, flirting with him. By the way, he had a clean-shaven head and she would direct her jokes toward him, then go over and rub him on his head, and at one point sat in his lap. Throughout her act he never moved or reacted to anything she said or did, which would make the audience scream with laughter.

The next act was introduced and a trio of young ladies performed. Unaware of the act before theirs, they flirted with the gentleman as well. The young male comedian who followed them included the senior into his act too. As he concluded, he asked the others who accompanied the senior why he couldn't get a response or reaction from him, and they replied, "He doesn't understand English, and he only speaks German."

As he left the stage, I stood up to rush Vickie's dressing room to inform her of the situation out front. Now there was no printed program for the show, so as I stood up to go to her dressing room the announcer called her name, "Ladies and gentlemen, Vickie Sykes." She briskly walked out of one entrance while I ran through another. When I realized that I couldn't get to her in time, I remained standing in the rear of the building, trying to get her attention by waving my arms back and forth, signaling to make her understand NOT to try to interact with the bald-headed gentleman.

Of course, I failed in my attempt. People around me were laughing at me so hard that they totally missed her first song. I jumped, I pointed, and I waved. Nothing worked. She totally ignored me.

While into her third song, like everyone else, she began to flirt. At this point I stopped all of my motions and gestures. She rubbed his head, she ran her hand across his shoulder but he never moved or uttered a word. The audience could see that she didn't know what to do. At the conclusion of her final song, the people stood and gave her a standing ovation, and as the people clapped, the young man walked up to Vickie and told her that the elderly gentleman only spoke

German. Vickie laughed all the way home, not about the gentleman but at me waving and jumping!

The Jokes On Me

A Tribute to Eddie Murphy

My second husband and I hadn't been married but a few short weeks when he called my office one day and offered to take me to lunch. Of course I agreed and the time was set for 11:45 a.m. that day. He arrived at 11:40 and off we went, with all the ladies in the office snickering and teasing me about my new marriage.

As we walked down Wilshire Blvd., trying to agree where to eat lunch, we passed a young man in a telephone booth. My husband glanced at him as we passed, not saying a word. As we continued to walk further, we saw a lot of commotion ahead of us. It appeared to be a location site for a movie being filmed. We were right but wondered what celebrities would be on the set. My husband felt that it was someone big in the industry because there were so many trailers and very large ones at that.

We went on to have a really good lunch at a nearby Thai restaurant. On our way back we passed the movie set and the same young man was in the telephone booth again, a short distance from the largest trailer. At that point, my husband stopped and said, "Wait, I think I know that young man!" He walked up closer to him, leaving me a few feet away, saying something that made the guy smile and say hello. I continued to just stand there and wonder who he was and what they could possibly be talking about.

My husband walked back over to me and asked if I would just wait there for a few seconds, and he would be right back. I agreed and stood near the phone booth like a mannequin, watching as he left me to walk over to the trailer with the young man. As they entered it a security guard who was nearby, no doubt on duty, watched also and smiled at me. So I'm standing there wondering why he was smiling. My husband stepped out of the trailer after a short time and beckoned for me to come to the trailer. I walked over thinking, okay what's going on? He reached out his hand to help me into the trailer.

When I entered, there sat Eddie Murphy. I stood in disbelief, with a look of Wow, on my face and said, "It's Eddie Murphy." He smiled and was very cordial as he offered me a seat, and the fun began. Well the young man in the phone booth was his brother, Charlie Murphy (it was before cell phones). My husband recognized him from his teaching days at Roosevelt High in New York. Charlie suggested that he come into the trailer to say hello to Eddie.

Eddie was on site filming Beverly Hills Cop I or II, I can't remember which. Anyway it was the scene where he was thrown out of a plate-glass front door.

Let me go back to the trailer. Once I was introduced as my husband's new wife, Eddie took over the conversation. He began to tell me all about my husband's escapades while he taught at Roosevelt High. Eddie described his platform shoes so closely, I could actually see them. He talked about his huge afro and the cool sports car that he drove.

He went on to say how all the kids really liked him. He was just a few years older than they were and so cool. My husband had attended Roosevelt High and was the captain of the basketball team a few years earlier. Playing on the same high school team with "Dr. J" made everyone on the team popular. Then him being the team's captain really made him all that! He received a scholarship to play college ball and returned to New York after a few years to teach at his alma mater.

Eddie and Charlie shared a lot with me that day. One story in particular was about one of my husband's girlfriends at the time that came up to the school, located his sports car and busted out the windows. They said that the kids teased him for weeks after that incident. That really should have been an immediate warning for me, but it wasn't. I was in LOVE!

We laughed and had a great 20 minute visit. As we prepared to leave, Eddie gave my husband his L.A. phone number and asked if he would stay in touch.

I was late getting back to work, but after my co-workers listened to my story on how I spend my lunch hour, they were understanding and immediately rushed out of the office hoping to see him as well. I've liked him ever since, nope not my husband, but Eddie Murphy. After all he tried to warn me!

Do I Get On the Bus?

Not having to use public transportation for over forty years, since junior high school, was a very new process for me. I married in 2002 and moved from the inner city of Los Angeles to West Covina, a neighboring suburb approximately 25 miles away. Experiencing one year of commuting by bus, allowed me to write this story.

Early in the year one afternoon, a bus driver drove so rapidly that when he did stop he announced over the speaker, "Thank you for flying _bus name intentionally blank_ . Hope you enjoyed your flight and please join us again." Everyone exited the bus in total exasperation.

Several weeks later, en-route home a teenage boy got on the bus. Since the bus was very crowded he had to stand, which was immediately in front of me. When his shirt flung open, there was his gun. Please don't ask what caliber, I know nothing about them. Of course my mind went immediately to, okay he is going to rob everyone on the bus and then kill us all, with one gun mind you! I was shaking all the way to my stop, but of course he never bothered anyone. Later I told a girlfriend about the incident and she laughed and said, "You were probably the only one on the bus without a gun!"

Several weeks later, early one morning, after riding for about 15 minutes I looked into the driver's rear view mirror and noticed that he was nodding at the wheel. All I could think to do was to pray in a big hurry.... Lord, send angels, wake him up, don't let anyone hit us, don't allow him to hit anyone! When we stopped about halfway to my destination, the driver got off the bus and began to walk around it as if he was checking the tires. I felt that I was the only one that knew the real deal. He was looking for a cup of caffeine!

I was praying while he was walking. When he got back on the bus I went up to him and asked if he was ill. He smiled and simply said, "I'm just tired." I have been driving since 11:00 p.m. last evening. Now it was 7:00 a.m. I told him that I could see that he was having a problem and that I was praying for him. He thanked me and began to quote the bible scripture, "When two are gathered in my name, I will be in the midst."

One day I was sitting in the front section reserved for senior citizens because there were no other available seats. A senior veteran got on the bus and stood but began to yell, "It's too bad that people don't respect senior vets today. I quietly said, "Sir here's a seat right here next to me." But as he sat next to me he continued to complain for the next ten minutes, speaking very loudly to everyone on the bus, but no one in particular.

The next week I encountered Mr. Hungry. He was a gentleman on the bus who was apparently very hungry. He was neatly dressed and quite handsome. Out of a grocery bag he pulled out a tortilla, a slice of bologna, the small packages of mustard you can usually get from a deli and neatly made himself a sandwich. I was so amazed at the time he took to prepare the sandwich that I actually wanted a bite of it.

Please keep in mind that the other passengers on the bus seemed to be so into whatever they were doing that they missed the experience of watching him. I couldn't help but wonder if I am an extremely observant person or just nosey.

One day I got on the bus and there was a lady bus driver who was usually okay, but this day would be different. A lady got on the bus behind me and the driver offered a ticket. When the passenger snatched the ticket out of the driver's hand, the yelling began. All the men on the bus woke up and you could see it in their eyes, Cat Fight, Cat Fight! I was so embarrassed. Finally things settled down. At the stop where the tickets are collected, the bus driver decided to snatch the ticket from the passenger's hand. That started the battle all over again. They both became pugnacious and very loud. I was so embarrassed again. I kept my head down, ashamed of their behavior. It seemed like forever getting to that particular passengers stop. I was so thankful. I was beginning to wonder if I would have to finish the route! Like I can drive a bus!

Let me leave you with some tips on bus etiquette:

Always observe pecking order. Get on the bus in the order in which you arrived at the depot or stop. If you try to break the line, be prepared for an arrest.

Never ask a man to let you have his seat, because if he doesn't automatically get up when you get on, and they usually don't, then you know that he's just a man and not a gentleman.

Always be prepared to get up when a handicapped person enters the bus, if you happen to be sitting in the handicapped or senior section of the bus or just expect a good cussing' out.

Pay close attention to your bus driver as you enter the bus. He may be intoxicated, sleepy or just plain crazy. Listen for the voice of the spirit. He'll let you know if you should get on the bus.

CHAPTER SIX

GET SERIOUS

A Friend in Need
or a Friend in Deed?

It was my first week back to work after being home for a year. Yes, back to Corporate America. I reported to work on a Monday morning to learn that the office would be moving several blocks away, to Third Street and Grand Avenue in one week. I had been hired as an administrative assistant for a national thrift. Two weeks prior to the starting date of my new job, I received a juror summons requesting that I report for jury duty in three weeks. My notice required me to report to the courts on the first day of our move into our new facility.

I arrived at the Los Angeles downtown court house, earlier than most on Monday morning, a bit afraid even though I had served several years prior. I was given a number and told to remain in a waiting room until my number was called.

As I waited my mind drifted into what I call "the wonders:" I wonder if this, I wonder if that. My mind went to; I wonder if I will run into any celebrities while

I'm here, who were summoned like me. Then, in walked Mr. Henry Winkler, "The Fonz." He sat for a while and was eventually called by the clerk. Apparently he had asked to be released on that particular day. I could hear him requesting a later date and I assumed his work schedule wouldn't allow him to remain.

I was finally called that afternoon after returning from an hour and a half lunch break. In the courtroom sat a Black man with a very long full beard and a shaved head. He was neatly dressed in what appeared to be new clothes. He wore a light blue shirt with open collar, long sleeves, dark trousers without a belt and his shoes were dark and polished. He sat quietly next to a young White female district attorney. He had been accused of the homicide of a male transient, apparently residing in downtown Los Angeles.

The man in the courtroom, the defendant, was a transient as well, homeless and lived on the streets of downtown Los Angeles. I watched his every move during the time I was in the courtroom with him and his attorney. Every time she got up to panel a juror, he would pull her chair out for her. I thought to myself would a murderer be so kind?

She and the other attorneys questioned juror after juror. It was obvious that some wanted to remain on the case while others like me, were nervous and wanted out.

It wasn't until Tuesday late afternoon that my name was called to be paneled as a juror.

By the time they got to me, I had all of my reasons together in my mind as to why I should not be a juror. My brother-in-law was a criminal attorney, my former husband was a probation officer, and my major in school was criminal justice. I was a minister and administrator in my church and felt that I would not make a good judge. Also I knew I would fight to the end, doing all that I could do to convince the other jurors that this person was innocent, regardless to the amount of incriminating evidence presented. I just felt he was.

Okay, so now I felt I was ready to fight my way out of the juror's box. Approximately 30 of us in the waiting room were called by our numbers and the selection process began. I was one of the last to be called to the witness stand to be questioned by the attorneys. When my name was finally called, they began to take me through the six to ten questions they had asked approximately 20 people prior to calling me.

I was asked if I had any relatives that served in the field of criminal justice. I went through my entire prepared spill on that question and went on to volunteer the information that I served as a minister and administrator in my church and felt that I would not make a good juror. It appeared as though they did not listen to me at all. They kept me on the case as a potential juror for at least an hour, before excusing me from the jury panel and the case altogether. I left as quickly as I could, hoping they would not change their minds before I could get out of the courtroom.

I reported to my new job location the following Wednesday and Thursday, helping each day to organize our new offices. But on Friday morning as I crossed the island on Third and Grand, I spotted a gentleman who appeared to be a bit startled and staring at me. As I walked closer to him, fear set in and I began to think, what must I say, or should I say anything?

It was the guy who was being held for murder that I had seen in the courtroom several days before. He had been released and apparently that was his corner, or should I say his location to ask for alms. My brain went crazy with "the wonders." Would he remember me as one who was a potential juror on his case? Wonder if he is going to say anything to me? What was I to do? There were just a few people on the street and no one directly in front of the building I was to enter. By now, my blood pressure was rising and I could feel my heart beating really fast.

As I approached him, approximately three or four feet away, he began to talk to me. Hello, he said, "You were the lady in the courtroom that refused to judge me. Lady do you realize how many people were there wanting to judge me? I want to thank you for what you did." I was flabbergasted and didn't know exactly what to say. Finally I spoke and asked, "They let you go?" He replied, "Yes, they had to. I didn't kill anyone." I quickly apologized and said, "I'm sorry, I mean, they found you innocent?" Again he replied, "Yes, they had to, I didn't kill anyone."

I smiled and thanked God as I left, that things went as well as they did, and he thanked me again as I said, "I never thought of you as a murderer the entire time I was in the courtroom."

Every work day for the next two years I stopped and talked with Mr. Ernest Adams. He would share his ups and downs with me and I would offer him money and ask if he had enough to eat. Rarely would he accept the dollar bills I offered him. He explained that he received a small check but it wasn't enough to get an apartment in the area. He wanted to remain downtown because he knew the ins and outs of the area, like where to go for shelter—outdoor shelter that is— and what grocery stores to go to in the evenings that would be tossing vegetables and fruits for the day, etc.

I would give him food that was left over from meetings and luncheons that we had in our office.

No one was a stranger to him. Sometimes I would see him doing little things for people and they would give him money. If he didn't need any money at that time he wouldn't accept it, but there were several people that would insist on him accepting their gift in exchange for him being of some assistance to them.

If he didn't know your name he would make one up for you like, pretty black, pretty lady, tall gorgeous, etc. Early on I told him that I was a minister in my church, hoping that he would keep that in mind and never get out of line. We became good friends. At home I would tell my husband and sons about Mr. Ernest practically daily. They began to inquire about him if I wouldn't mention him. "Mom, did you see Mr. Ernest today?" they would ask.

I can recall my husband and sons driving me to work one day and we passed him on the street. I said, "Hey, there's Mr. Ernest." They yelled out of the window, "Hello Mr. Ernest." He smiled, with that one missing front tooth, and waved, later asking me, if that was my family that waved at him and yelled his name.

Mr. Ernest would stop me and want to talk and tell me stories of how people wouldn't want to wait on him in restaurants because of the way he was dressed. He pushed a grocery cart containing three pieces of luggage and many other items on top. I got up enough nerve to ask him one day what was in the luggage? He was proud to show me that they were filled with books. He said he really liked to read and I was shocked.

One day as I approached him, he handed me a note and he said, "Rev. Price I use to prepare taxes, please give this to your tax man." I wondered what, my tax man? He had written a note indicating that I had supported him for over a year and that he should be considered a write off for me.

I thought of him that day and wondered how such a guy could end up in this condition. I later heard that he had moved to Los Angeles years before to play professional ball and things just didn't work out.

Several months later he asked how he could contact me and said that he was going to contact his mother and ask her to send me money because I had been very nice to her son. He said that she was wealthy and lived back east. It was really strange because I was really in need at the time. The thought alone was just kind enough for me that day.

On the way home one day, I heard on the news that a homeless man had been beaten practically to death by two teenage boys, and that he resided downtown Los Angeles. I wondered if it was Mr. Ernest. Later I found out that it was indeed him by overhearing a conversation between people walking down the street near my job.

Months passed before anyone heard or said anything about him. One day I walked into the post office on the ground level of our building and Mr. Ernest was in line. When I walked in, we recognized each other, hugged and said hello. I told him I had thought of him often and wondered if was alive. He then took off his cap and showed me the stitches in his head from the blows he received from the two boys that attacked him.

It actually looked like a road map to me. I told him that I was glad to know he was alive. We shook hands and parted and I haven't seen Ernest since that day. That was four years ago.

When walking to my office from my car each morning, which was about a seven minute walk, I always felt a sense of security knowing Ernest was nearby. I believed that if he heard of a lady who fell in the street and broke a leg, or a lady was mugged, he would be one of the first who would come to see if it was me. I thought of him as my friend indeed!

Zacheus Sees and Hears President Obama

My husband Mark and I had longed to have an opportunity to one day see President Obama in person. When we heard he was coming to Los Angeles, we began to make plans. I asked for the day off from the doctor I worked for. She agreed and the planning began. We arrived at the University of Southern California, approximately 10 minutes from our home around 8:30 a.m. Mark had scoped out the route via Google from home, so he knew where to park, which was three blocks from USC's Vermont Avenue gate. We stood in line with ten's of thousands until 10:45 a.m. It was very orderly and nice.

Finally we were allowed into the quad area which accommodated about 25 thousand people. We stood until 1:30 p.m. like sardines, waiting for President Obama to arrive. He had actually arrived and was having lunch with God knows who on campus. We did see the helicopter flying over and thought he must be inside. Jamie Foxx served as host of the rally with political dignitaries on hand speaking in hopes of gaining our votes. Those present were Jerry Brown, Barbara Boxer, L.A.'s Mayor Villaraigosa, Kamala Harris and others.

It was so hot, that everyone had come out of their morning gear, wishing they had left their coats and umbrellas in their cars. As soon as President Obama got up to speak, Mark grabbed my hand and blocked his way out of the crowd, moving quickly and saying "coming through, excuse us please, and repeating it over and over." Everyone was on the same level, no slopes, and no hills. It was horrible. You couldn't see a thing! Heads, shoulders everywhere, to our left, right, front and back. One lady passed out who was standing near us, but he pushed his way through the crowd until we were able to get out of the mess.

Lord I was so glad...finally able to breath again!

He walked directly over to the largest speaker he could find to just listen to him. I asked him to remain at that specific spot as I walked behind the crowd hoping to get a glimpse of the President's face. I finally got a spot. Yep gooood looking! Boy, O Boy, and his speech was awesome. The man is just good, what can I say?

When I returned to where I had left Mark, I could not find him. Keep in mind that the President was speaking—he was saying stuff like.... "If you want to go forward you must put the car in D for drive—D (Democrats). If you want to go in reverse put it in R (for Republican). He's just good!

Still looking for Mark....I happened to look up and there he stood on the tallest stand that they had built to hold the speaker monitors. Not only could he see but he could hear every word that was being spoken by the President. Others were sitting on the stand but only Mark was standing. He had the best spot in the entire quad. All I could think of was Zacheus climbing up the tree to see Jesus.

We left USC and went to dinner. Following dinner we shopped at Trader Joe's, which happened to be the place Mark first saw me. Huh, just thought about that. While leaving Trader Joe's, because of his experience working in transportation, Mark knew exactly where to go to see the President's plane. We had just missed him but saw the huge carriers that contain his secret service equipment. As we left the area his motorcade passed us, but President Obama had already left en-route to his next stop....LAS VEGAS. What a day!

Yep...one thing off my bucket list!

CHAPTER SEVEN

MY GRANDSON
– PRECIOUS GEMS

Alphabets

My four year old grandson, Jordan came to visit me one day. I had purchased a deck of alphabet cards, the ones with photos of items on one side and alphabets on the other.

I asked him if he would like to play with the set of cards with me. He happily and hurriedly responded, "Yes, grandmother." I pulled card after card from the deck. To my surprise, he knew every card except the photo of an apron, but who wears aprons in the kitchen any more? I had no idea that he would know everyone of the letters as well as the photos representing each letter, except for the apron.

I began to question him as to how he knew all of this.

I asked, "Do you have cards like this at home?" He replied, "No."

I asked, "Did mommy teach you these letters? Again he replied, "No."

I asked, "Did daddy teach you the items on the cards from pictures from one of your books at home?" He replied, "No."

I continued to question him. "Did you learn some of the letters from watching television?" "No," he said but beginning to show signs of becoming annoyed with my questioning. He was looking around, swinging his legs, no longer really into what I'm asking.

In my frustration, I finally asked, "Well how did you learn all the alphabets and items on these cards?"

His response was, "Jesus told me."

That ended Grand mommy's interrogation. Case closed!

It Won't Work

I was working 35 miles from home in the summer of 2006 and would ride the freeway flyer to work daily after parking my car at the Park n Ride section of the Westfield Mall.

My 4-year-old grandson, Jordan wanted to spend the weekend with me and in order to do so; he had to be dropped off at my job late Friday evening. We would ride the bus to get to my car. My concern was, would he be able to ride for 30 to 40 minutes without having a need to go to the restroom. His mother assured me that he would be okay as long as I remembered to take him just before leaving my job.

He was dropped off around 5:00 p.m. on a Friday. He used the restroom prior to our walk to the bus stop which was about two blocks away.

When we got on the bus, the passengers were surprised to see him because this particular bus rarely had children passengers. It was normally filled with middle-aged people who lived in the suburbs but worked downtown Los Angeles. I could feel the tension as we boarded the bus. People were tired from a long work week and I'm sure were hoping for peace and quiet during their ride home.

I felt we would be okay because this was going to be his first bus ride and he was okay and enjoyed every minute of it. We sat at the very front, near the bus driver on the side bench seating. Jordan never said a word during the first twenty minutes. He would just sit, swing his legs, hold on to his toy car and look around at the passengers and the signs inside the bus.

Approximately 20 minutes into the ride, he looked up at me and said, "Grandmother I need to use it." Fear immediately set in. I could not believe that those five little words, I need to use it, could turn me into a wreck. Well they did. All I could think about was him wetting the seat, his clothes, and the bus driver putting me off the bus twenty minutes away from my regular stop. Thoughts kept coming and I had him stand up then sit on his coat, just in case.

I asked him if he could hold it. As he answered, "Yes," he placed his toy car on the bench next to him and placed both hands over his private area. He literally thought I meant to hold IT!

We rode another twenty minutes with him holding IT! I continued to ask him, as I prayed, if he could continue to hold it and he would nod yes. It seemed as though it took an hour to get to our stop. When we finally arrived, I rushed him off the bus and literally had him run with me to my car. I pulled him between my car and the next one over and pulled his pants down as fast as I could. He grabbed IT and held it out facing the rear of my car. After a few seconds, he looked up at me and said, "It won't work."

I don't know if he was afraid someone might see him, or if it was too cold. So I pulled his pants up, buckled him into the car and drove home wondering if he thought in his little mind that it was actually broken.

I still can't figure it out, in my old mind, because as soon as we got home, it worked!

I'm Here

My son Channing brought my four year old grandson Jordan over to spend the Fourth of July with me. The holiday was going to fall on a Friday, so he was dropped off late afternoon Thursday. I decided I wanted to barbeque, (something I knew very little about), on Thursday so I could spend all day Friday visiting with Jordan.

He assisted me with bringing out the coals, wood chips, utensils, containers of meat, etc. Once he saw that I was pretty settled he asked if he could play basketball in the entryway of the front door. I agreed and besides, he had been so helpful.

His dad had bought him the miniature basketball set that hooks onto the top of a door frame and he loved it. I can't think of any other thing he preferred playing with.

I cooked on the patio as he played basketball in the entryway. Whenever I was on the patio, I was unable to see him, because there was a wall that blocked my direct view of that section of the house. So I began to play with him by singing, "Jordan, where are you?" He would respond, "I'm here." I would sing, "I can't see you," then he would try to emulate my vocals by replying, "I'm here." His singing was my way of being assured that he was okay. We went on like this for a while, singing to each other.

I finally finished cooking (barbequing), after almost setting a small tree on my patio on fire. At one point I was inhaling so much of the smoke that I began to cough very hard. Jordan decided that he would come to see about me asking, "Grandmother, are you okay?" I had to laugh.

We had a great visit that afternoon. After all the work had been done and he was tired of playing basketball, we read some of his favorite books together. Some words he knew, others he learned that day. The next day was the fourth. We slept in that morning, ate barbeque and played all afternoon. When it was time for him to leave, I became saddened as we hugged and said good bye. I knew that I would miss him, since he was my first and only grandchild. With his parents' schedule and mine, and living such a distance apart, it was difficult getting to see him very often.

The next morning, I woke up thinking of Jordan and how much we enjoyed our holiday. As I walked to the kitchen to prepare breakfast, the spirit spoke a profound statement to me. This is what the Lord said. "Do you remember asking Jordan 'Where are you?" My response was, "Yes." His voice went on to say, "Just like you couldn't see him, you can't see me, but you could hear him and if you would listen closely enough you'll hear me, because, I'm Here." My mind was blown.

About the Author

Ruthell Cook Price, is a native of Los Angeles, California. She and her husband Mark now resides in Atlanta, GA.

She received her Bachelor of Science Degree in Criminal Justice from California State University Los Angeles.

She is the proud mother of Channing Cook Holmes, a Renowned tap dancer, award winning choreographer and percussionist. Her youngest son Lladon is currently a student at Morehouse College.

She has served for 35 years at Harvest Tabernacle Bible Church as, Associate Minister, Board Member, Special Events Coordinator and Executive Assistant to the Senior Pastor.

She was assistant coordinator for the initial Los Angeles NAACP's ACT-SO Program.

Ruth has worked in the field of music as a studio singer and contractor and has recorded with Stevie Wonder, the late Charles Veal Jr. (violinist) and others. She is a member of the Musicians Union.

She was employed in the banking industry for over 27 years, serving in the Department of Community Affairs.

Ruth was inducted into John C. Fremont High School's Hall of Fame in 2001, acknowledged as a professional in the banking industry and for her volunteer efforts in formulating a gospel choir at her alma mater.

As a contributor to the "Chicken Soup for the Soul" series, Ruth is enjoying her new venture of writing. She is also an inspirational speaker with a drive to encourage those that are weary in well doing.

She can be contacted via email: ruthellcookprice@gmail.com.

Ruthell Cook Price

Proceeds

Portions of the proceeds through sales of this publication will benefit "Heart of Harvest," a non profit organization that was organized by Ruth in 1997. "Heart of Harvest" provides funds for families in crises and books for college students. The organization was formed through the assistance of Donna Avery, Sharon Swendell, Brenda Piggee, Brenda Freeman, Darnell Washington and Jo Ann Newton, under the auspices of the California Harvest Tabernacle Church, Inc.